CRITICAL THEORY FOR SOCIAL WORK
A Simple Introduction

Joe Whelan

First published in Great Britain in 2025 by

Policy Press, an imprint of
Bristol University Press
University of Bristol
1–9 Old Park Hill
Bristol
BS2 8BB
UK
t: +44 (0)117 374 6645
e: bup-info@bristol.ac.uk

Details of international sales and distribution partners are available at
policy.bristoluniversitypress.co.uk

British Library Cataloguing in Publication Data
A catalogue record for this book is available from the British Library

ISBN 978-1-4473-7168-7 paperback
ISBN 978-1-4473-7169-4 ePub
ISBN 978-1-4473-7170-0 ePdf

Cover design: Andy Ward
Front cover image: Alamy/Vlad Kochelaevskiy
Bristol University Press and Policy Press use environmentally responsible
print partners.
Printed and bound in Great Britain by CPI Group (UK) Ltd, Croydon, CR0 4YY

FSC
www.fsc.org
MIX
Paper | Supporting
responsible forestry
FSC® C013604

For my parents, Kevin and Lucinda

Contents

Contents

List of figures

About the author

Joe Whelan is a sociologist and social policy scholar, a qualified social worker and an Assistant Professor in the School of Social Work and Social Policy, Trinity College Dublin, the University of Dublin. Joe is a member of the Editorial Collective of the high-impact scholarly journal *Critical Social Policy*. Joe teaches critical theory to social work students. His ambition for learners taking any of the modules on which he teaches is that they would take what is introduced in the classroom and pursue it further in a self-directed way. He therefore tries to foster passion, interest, excitement and curiosity. As an educator, Joe also believes that there are many ways to connect students with learning that go beyond the traditional lecture format. In this respect, he uses music, literature, poetry and art in his teaching. Joe hopes that some of the approach he takes in the classroom is reflected in this book.

About this book and core learning outcomes

This is a book about thinking as opposed to doing. The purpose of this book is to introduce students to critical social theory and to the work of several theorists in simple terms and to show how the work of these theorists can be used to think about different aspects of social work. These theorists are not social work theorists per se and the theories they have developed are not social work practice theories. In other words, this is *not* a book that will tell you how to do social work, but it can help you think about it.

The inspiration for writing this book has come, in part, from teaching social work students about social theory and critical social theory in particular. Through this, I have found that when theory is introduced in a simple and accessible way, students generally enjoy studying it and enjoy using it to think about social work. This book will therefore allow students and other readers to gain some measure of familiarity with the theories and concepts described as based on the author's reading and interpretation and hopefully spur readers towards deepening their understanding and beginning their own journeys of interpretation. This point about interpretation is an important point and I make it to suggest that readers should not be put off by what can often seem like complex interpretations of social theory. Social theory is for *everyone*, not just intellectuals and academics. Social theory is also not something that should be thought of as having sharp edges that must 'lock' into place when using it. Rather, social theory is often blurry around the margins and can be used approximately. There is no test of exactness when using social theory to think about something like social work. On this basis, I would suggest to readers to forget about complexity or about fears of being 'right' or 'wrong' if they have any and simply take what they find useful and leave the rest. If you as a reader find a concept useful for thinking about social work, then that's great. If this spurs you to deeper reflection, even better. If you happen to find any of the interpretations in this book useful, then I will have done my job.

Though intended to be short, simple and accessible, the aim of this book is undoubtedly grand in scale. In this respect, it is hoped to do here for social work what C. Wright Mills once did for sociology; that is, to begin to develop the social work imagination of the reader by breaking down that which can at first seem impenetrable and rendering it understandable and therefore useful. With this in mind, the book in your hands or on your screen is not rooted in a specific context or jurisdiction. The book also aims to reapproach the 'macro' in social work by striving to develop thinking and foster engagement with some of the big picture issues that are affecting social work as a global profession. In a profession that has become evermore micro personal in nature, this is an important task and thinking theoretically about social work can aid with this.

Throughout the book, text boxes explain key terms or note key people, which appear in bold. Each theorist is introduced and some of their theories and concepts are sketched out very simply before being briefly related to social work. Depending on the theorist, in some cases concepts and theories are each separately related to social work within a chapter and in other cases what has been introduced is related, as a whole, to social work. Each chapter ends with an exercise box containing questions/prompts to encourage you to think further. For those who wish to go beyond the text, additional resources including podcasts, YouTube clips and, of course, further reading materials are signposted.

The theorists presented in the book, though they may have had very different views on many things, are not presented in opposition to one another. Rather, their ideas are described independently and their usefulness for social work explored. Moreover, this is not a book that enters into an overt critique of the works discussed. Rather, theorists and ideas are presented at face value, related to social work, and readers are then free to make up their own minds as to the usefulness or not of what has been presented. Moreover, the theorists covered in this book do not form an exhaustive list by any means and therefore readers are encouraged to take what they learn here and apply it as broadly as possible. In this respect, the book has several core learning outcomes, which are as follows:

• Readers will be able to distinguish between concepts and theory generally.
• Readers will have a good understanding of what generally characterises theory associated with traditional modernity and what characterises theory associated with postmodernity.
• Readers will be able take their understanding of how to use theory to think about social work and apply it to the work of theorists not covered in this text.
• Readers will be able to use the theories and concepts introduced in the text as tools that allow them to reflect deeply on practice.

These learning outcomes will be readdressed in the final summary chapter. In terms of how to approach the book, it is of course best read cover to cover. However, from Chapter 3 onwards the text begins introducing individual theorists and so readers can choose to dip in and out of the text. However, I would recommend that all readers engage with the first two chapters before reading further as these are written to help build an understanding of theory and also help to position the theorists that are covered in the remainder of the book.

Resources for lecturers can be found on the Bristol University Press website at: https://policy.bristoluniversitypress.co.uk/critical-theory-for-social-work.

1

Introduction to theory: theorising social work

Social work as a practical and applied activity is about doing *and* thinking. In fact, practising social work requires a great deal of thought before, during and after practice. **Paulo Freire** might have described this type of activity, which requires both thought and action, as 'praxis'. Praxis is a reflective approach to thinking and doing. It is an ongoing process of moving between practice and theory with each continually informing and hopefully enhancing the other (Freire, 1985). Social work is distinct from many other occupations because it requires you to think as deeply as possible about what you are doing and why. Through deciding to become a social worker, you will also be asked to think about the profession of social work itself, how it came to be, how it came to be the way it is, what is good and progressive about social work and what could perhaps be challenged or changed. Thinking through such important questions can be difficult and requires an academic grounding. Social work as a profession draws heavily from social sciences like sociology, psychology, social policy and economics. Social work is also an academic discipline in its own right, with an expansive literature on social work theory, values and skills. This book is a book about theory. There are many books about social work theory that cover practice theories like task-centred approaches or systems theory. However, this book is different. Social work practice theories are not covered here and instead this book covers the work of a range of theorists whose ideas can be useful in helping you to do the thinking that forms such a core component of modern social work practice. Therefore, social theory and, more particularly, critical social theory are at the core of this book.

> **Paulo Freire** (19 September 1921 to 2 May 1997) was a Brazilian educator and philosopher. His most influential work, *Pedagogy of the Oppressed* was and continues to be hugely influential in many fields including in social work education and practice.

Defining terms

Given that this is a book about social theory and critical social theory and not about practice theories, the first thing to do here is to define these terms. Thorpe (2017: 5) describes social theory in the following way:

> In a general sense, social theory is a body of knowledge aimed at making sense of human life, both from a broad historical perspective and specifically too in the forms it takes in society today. Social theory

is made up of concepts from a range of academic disciplines. Of these disciplines, social theory is aligned most closely with sociology.

There are a few important things to take from Thorpe's (2017) definition. Firstly, Thorpe writes about social theories potentially helping us to make sense of the forms of human life. For the purpose of this book, the forms of human life we are most interested in making sense of are those either directly impacted by or otherwise impactful for social work. Thorpe (2017) also writes about how social theory is made up of concepts and so it is important at the outset to distinguish between what is meant by a concept and what is meant by a theory as these can often be used interchangeably. There are many complex and contested explanations of concepts and theories and of the differences between each. For our purposes, the following simple explanations, which are threaded through with an example, will be in use:

- **A concept** is a simple tool to help aid understanding. To be able to understand the world and each other, we need to be able to share concepts. So, for example, if I write that I own a pet cat, you will implicitly understand the concept of 'pet' from what I have written. Concepts are not definitions because they go beyond language and include practices; people who speak different languages understand the concept 'pet' even if they speak, write or pronounce it differently. In other words, language and vocabulary are what we use to define and communicate about the concept 'pet'; however, what it means to have a pet exists in a set of practices. To quote the linguist and philosopher, Ferdinand de Saussure: 'Among all the individuals that are linked together by speech, some sort of average will be set up: all will reproduce – not exactly of course, but approximately – the same signs united with the same concepts' (de Saussure, 1959/2011: 13). Drawing on de Saussure here we may take signs to refer to language or words that we unite with shared concepts in order to communicate. Concepts are also distinctly human; no species other than humans is likely to understand the concept 'pet'.
- **A theory** goes beyond helping us to understand the world and each other for the purposes of communication and attempts to explain it or some part of it. To stick with the example of pets, we may implicitly understand the idea of pet ownership, but do we understand how pet ownership came about, what the particular social conditions that gave rise to pet ownership were and what pet ownership consists of today? Moreover, why do people own pets? Why do people own specific types of pets? Why do people in specific geographical areas own specific types of pets? Why do people from different class backgrounds own different types of pets? A theory or theories may be needed to help explain some or all of this. We can therefore also distinguish between, 'grand theories', 'middle-range theories' and 'micro theories'. A grand theory in this instance may seek to explain pet ownership as a social phenomenon on a grand scale, so that it might present us with a theory of pet ownership in France taking in historical and modern conditions and the differences between

each. A middle-range theory may attempt to do something smaller and might present us with a theory of dog ownership in a working-class suburb in Paris, focusing on how particular breeds of dog are used as status symbols and offering a theory of how and why this came about. A micro theory will be concerned with something smaller again and may explore how a small sample of dog owners experience the process of boarding their dogs at a specific kennel in a specific suburb on a specific street in Paris. Theories may be advanced through conducting research of different types, and it is possible to both test a theory through doing research or to arrive at a theory through doing research. For all of this to be possible, remember, we need the concept of 'pet'.

If we take what has been presented above and use it to think about social work, the usefulness should be clear. Let's take the example of 'foster care'. As a concept, foster care is immediately understandable at a basic level to most people and across languages. This means we can communicate about it with each other to some degree. But what if we want to understand where foster care came from, how it came about, what kinds of people offer foster care and what kinds of people enter foster care? For this, we will need to access relevant literature and see what theories about foster care are out there. Perhaps somebody does this and finds that there is a gap in knowledge or that the theories on offer are dissatisfying. Perhaps this person has a theory themselves and decides to do some research to see if it can be affirmed. Perhaps somebody does some research on foster care and the results add to existing theory or help to develop new ones. It is possible to run through this example with multiple aspects of social work, including social work as a whole. For the most part, the theorists discussed in the chapters to follow will have advanced grand theories. However, the building blocks of these grand theories will be made up of many interlocking concepts that allow us to communicate about the theories and that come together to give the theories their explanatory power.

Critical social theory

Having now grappled with the idea of social theory, our next job becomes distinguishing general social theory from critical social theory. Critical social theory is often first and foremost associated with the famous **Frankfurt School** or Institute

> Formally founded in 1923, by Carl Grünberg, the **Frankfurt School** is a school of social theory and critical philosophy associated with the Institute for Social Research, founded at Goethe University Frankfurt in 1923. The term 'Frankfurt School' goes beyond the bounds of the institute and describes the works of those who were associated with the school. The linking of critical theory with the Frankfurt School stems from the emphasis of the work being done by scholars associated with the school, which was generally concerned with studying the effects of capitalist ideology, mass culture, consumerism and technology on a subject's consciousness.

> **Positivism** is an approach to social science that uses the principles of natural science to study society and to arrive at knowledge claims.

> **Max Horkheimer** (14 February 1895 to 7 July 1973) was a German philosopher and sociologist and, along with Theodor Adorno, was a prominent critical theorist of the Frankfurt School.

for Social Research. This is not surprising given that the emphasis for those whose work was and is associated with the school was very much couched in critique and stemmed from a broad dissatisfaction with mainstream '**positivist**' social science, which did much to explore social conditions but had little concern with challenging or changing them. The project of the Frankfurt School was very much concerned with the emancipatory potential of the social sciences. Indeed, in setting out the differences between traditional and critical theory, **Max Horkheimer** (1972/2002: 215) describes the critical theorist as someone who fosters:

> a dynamic unity with the oppressed class, so that his presentation of societal contradictions is not merely an expression of the concrete historical situation but also a force within it to stimulate change.

The critical theorist then is concerned not just with theory but with emancipation, liberation and change. As such, the tradition of critique arising from the Frankfurt School owed much to Karl Marx who is covered here further on.

While the critical social theory of the Frankfurt School is important and two theorists associated with the school are included in this book, the conceptualisation of critical social theory offered here is much broader and includes the work of those who would not be associated with the Frankfurt School but who will have offered theories, thoughts and ideas with the goal of critique and emancipation at their core in different ways. Summing this up, the following definition by Callinicos (1999: 2) provides us with some building blocks:

> Critical social theory seeks to understand society as a whole; distinguishes between and makes generalizations about different kinds of society; is concerned in particular to analyse modernity, the social life, the forms of social life which have come to prevail first in the West and increasingly in the rest of the world over the past couple of centuries.

This definition by Callinicos (1999: 2) makes a useful starting point. A key distinction between it and the definition of general social theory given by Thorpe (2017) is that critical social theory is very much concerned with conditions and forms of social life as they are now or have recently been. This is because as well as offering explanation, critical social theory can seek to offer pathways towards change, although these are not always easy to discern as we will see. Nevertheless, it is impossible to change how history has been experienced but the here and now can be affected and so critical social theory can offer explanation to effect change. Finally, then, in distinguishing between social theory generally and critical social theory, I draw on Harvey (1990: 02) who notes that:

> The difference between critical approaches and noncritical approaches is not the difference between the presence and absence of critique, rather it is the difference between approaches in which critique is an integral part of the process and those in which it is peripheral.

For critical social theorists, critique is at the heart of the approach, not just a by-product. Therefore, the definition of critical social theory offered here is broad and encapsulates any social theory whereby critique of the object, whatever that object may be, is of central concern and whereby the concepts and theories offered have emancipatory potential. To nuance this further, we can also acknowledge that critical theory, in the main, has historically been drawn from western male thought, and therefore broadening our understanding of critical theory to include **indigenous knowledges and postcolonial perspectives**, while they are not covered extensively here, further deepens how we can conceive of critical theory.

In the next chapter, we begin the process of distinguishing between critical theory that might be considered traditional and associated with modernity and theory that might be associated with postmodernity or the postmodern. From there we will begin exploring the work of theorists. Because each theorist is presented in distinct terms, it is possible to dip in and out and while the ideal way to read the book is in order from Chapter 1 and from cover to cover, it is possible to also read a chapter discretely. However, as previously noted, it is strongly recommended that Chapter 2 is read as a precursor to all other chapters as this will certainly help to ground the work of the theorists who follow.

> **Indigenous knowledges** refers to the knowledges held by distinct social and cultural groups that share collective ancestral ties to the lands and natural resources where they live. **Postcolonial** in the context of theory is the critical academic study of the cultural, political and economic legacy of colonialism and imperialism.

For students: Exercise box 1

Think about an area of social work practice: this could be mental health social work, child protection social work or any other area of practice:

1. What are the key concepts in the area? Make a list of these.
2. What are some of the major theories in the area you have chosen? Do these theories simply explain, or do they explain and critique?

Further reading
- If you would like to read more social work practice theories, the following book by Malcom Payne makes an ideal starting point:
- Payne, M. (2020) *How to Use Social Work Theory in Practice – An Essential Guide*, Bristol: Policy Press.
- If you'd like to read more on thinking theoretically for social work, the following book by Paul Michael Garrett provides further reading:
- Garrett, P.M. (2018) *Social Work and Social Theory – Making Connections*, Bristol: Policy Press.

Chapter references

Callinicos, A. (1999) *Social Theory: A Historical Introduction*, Cambridge: Polity Press.

de Saussure, F. (1959/2011) *Course in General Linguistics*, New York: Columbia University Press.

Freire, P. (1985) *The Politics of Education: Culture, Power and Liberation*, Westport, CT: Bergin & Garvey Publishers, Inc.

Harvey, L. (1990) *Critical Social Research*, London: Unwin Hyman.

Horkheimer, M. (1972/2002) *Critical Theory: Selected Essays*, New York: Continuum.

Thorpe C. (2017) *Social Theory for Social Work: Ideas and Applications*, London: Routledge.

For instructors: A set of slides that accompany this chapter can be accessed through the book webpage: https://policy.bristoluniversitypress.co.uk/critical-theory-for-social-work.

2

Ways of knowing: traditional modernity and postmodernity

The world we live in is constantly subject to change and advancement with respect to what we know and accept to be true. This is true also of how we think about the world and perhaps even *what* we can think about it. On the one hand, it is possible to say that we know more now about more things than at any previous point in history. On the other hand, knowledge is much more contested now and there is a broad acknowledgement that not everyone experiences the world in the same way. In any case, how we know about and experience the world now is very different to how it was known about and experienced even 50 years ago. The task for this chapter is to differentiate between ways of knowing associated with what we call modernity and what we call postmodernity. However, before we discuss these terms and note their characteristics it is worth briefly introducing some concepts that can help when thinking about how we know what we know and how this has changed across time.

In *The Structure of Scientific Revolutions*, **Thomas Kuhn** (1962) attributes changes to what we know and to the ways we study about and view the world to what he calls 'paradigm shifts'. A paradigm shift occurs when the way we view something is fundamentally altered. For Kuhn (1962), a paradigm shift is a movement towards a more objective truth, a movement that replaces an older way of knowing. The new paradigm therefore offers a better explanation; an explanation that no longer fits with the old way of knowing. Kuhn (1962) was writing about shifts in the way science advances; however, the phrase 'paradigm shift' has undoubtedly taken on a broader and more general meaning to encapsulate shifts in the way we know about and understand things across many disciplines and aspects of life. Social work has arguably seen many paradigm shifts over the time of its existence; for example,

> **Thomas Kuhn**
> (18 July 1922 to
> 17 June 1996) was an
> American historian
> and philosopher of
> science whose 1962
> book *The Structure of
> Scientific Revolutions*
> was influential in
> both academic and
> popular circles,
> introducing the term
> 'paradigm shift',
> which has since
> become widely used.

the shift from individualising casework approaches towards more structural understandings or the shift from unregulated charity to professionalisation. Michel Foucault (1966: 162), who is covered in a chapter further on, introduced his version of the idea of *épistémè* in his book, *The Order of Things: An Archaeology of the Human Sciences* where he notes that:

> In any given culture and at any given moment, there is always only one épistémè that defines the conditions of possibility of all knowledge, whether expressed in a theory or silently invested in a practice.

Foucault later refined this assertion to suggest that more than one *épistémè* could persist at the same time. However, what is key in Foucault's (1966) assertion is his emphasis on how what it is possible to know is contingent on the conditions in a society or a culture at a given time. If we think about the fact that from about the start of the 5th century CE up until the beginning of the 15th century CE, knowledge, in the western world at least, was controlled almost exclusively through the Christian church, we can quickly realise that what it was possible for ordinary people to know during this period will have been very different to what it was possible for ordinary people to know during the Renaissance. Between the Renaissance and now, the possibilities for knowledge have of course shifted and shifted again. Social work will not have been immune to shifts in how we know what we know and as we move from modernity to postmodernity, we will see that social work can be characterised and thought about very differently depending on the lens.

Modernity

Modernisation refers to the transitional process of moving from 'traditional' or 'primitive' communities to modern societies. Adjacent to this, modernity can be summed up as the condition of being modern. Quite when modernity comes fully into being is widely contested but it is perhaps not too controversial to say that modernity encapsulates a condition of social existence that is significantly or even radically different to all past forms of human experience. Modernity encapsulates the vibrant, the modern and the new as opposed to the antiquated, the old, the traditional or the primitive. Modernity as a phase in human existence has been deeply influenced by and is arguably made up of a number of constituent parts that together led to the condition of being modern. These are explored below.

Key factors of modernity

The Enlightenment

The Enlightenment, otherwise referred to as the 'Age of Reason', begun roughly at the beginning of the 18th century. This was a period during which the ability to question and know about the world started to shift from something that was controlled by ideas about God and predominantly through the Christian church to one where it was possible for anyone to ask questions and to use reason to figure out and understand the world. Key aspects of Enlightenment thinking include:

• It is possible to know about the world: replacing gods with equations.
• It is practical to seek the 'truth'.

- The scientific method can be used to understand the world.
- Distinctions can be made between what its good and bad / right and wrong / beautiful and ugly.
- Examining ethics as a science can help us to arrive at conclusions about how best to live.
- It is possible for persons to become 'expert' in something; for example, health and medicine.

In his classic essay on 'Modernity, Postmodernity and Social Work', Howe (1994: 514) notes that:

> by the seventeenth century, the Scientific Revolution was encouraging people to be more curious about the world and the way it worked. Reason and mathematics, rational thought and systematic enquiry rather than the study of the divine Word would help humanity make sense of nature and society. Therefore, it was Reason which would lead to the truth and not Revelation.

Reason and a recognition of the ability to reason were core components of Enlightenment thinking. There was also a sense that not only was it possible to reason about the world, but it was possible to arrive at truth reflecting the pre-Enlightenment thought of figures like **Francis Bacon** who argued that the possibility of scientific knowledge should be based upon reasoning and careful observation. This in turn reflects what Howe (1994) has named as one of modernity's 'three great projects' in the form of the 'true'; the others being the 'beautiful' and the 'good'. Howe (1994: 518) also suggests that social work, in its own way, has pursued these three components of modernity 'as it attempts to bring about a pleasing quality of life and a just society by using the insights of the social sciences'. Suffice to say that the Enlightenment was an important period in giving shape to what would later be called modernity.

> **Francis Bacon** (22 January 1561 to 9 April 1626) was an English philosopher and politician. Bacon led the advancement of both natural philosophy and the scientific method, and his works remained influential even in the late stages of the Scientific Revolution.

The Renaissance

There were other things happening before and during the Enlightenment period that were also key in shaping modernity as the condition of being modern. The southern and later the northern Renaissance – which broadly encapsulate the 14th, 15th, 16th and 17th centuries – was a period during which new orders of beauty and truth were sought in art, architecture, politics and science. In many ways this was a project of looking back towards the period of classical antiquity for inspiration. However, it was also a project of moving forward towards new forms of knowing, understanding and interpreting. One of the most striking ways to illustrate the change to forms and order that happened during the Renaissance is to consider how art changed during this time. Classical art, or the art of ancient Greece and Rome, had sought to create convincing and realistic illusions. However, art and paintings during the Middle Ages from about 500 to 1400/1500 moved away from the forms associated with the art of antiquity. Artists had begun to abandon classical artistic techniques like shading and perspective, techniques that made the images appear real, and instead favoured flat representations of people and objects so that they looked only nominally like their subjects. Looking first to a piece of art created before the Renaissance began in earnest, we can take the example of Figure 2.1, the *Madonna and Child*, a tempera on wood by Berlinghiero who was active by 1228 and died by 1236.

This striking painting is flat and the figures within are strangely and unrealistically proportioned. While the figures within the scene are familiar from a cultural and religious perspective and while it is clear that we are looking at people, this is not a rendering of people who represent a realistic interpretation in any sense. If we next look at Figure 2.2, the *Lamentation (The Mourning of Christ)* by Giotto Di Bondone, 1305, a fresco painted on the walls of the Scrovegni Chapel in Padua in Italy, we see what would be described as a proto-Renaissance piece.

The focus of the painting is still firmly religious. The figures in this painting are still somewhat strange and certainly not hyper-realistic. Yet the proportions of the figures in the scene seem more natural. There is also a depth and perspective here that was absent from the previous example. This tells us very simply that as the Renaissance was in its formative stage and just beginning to bed in, new ways of portraying and interpreting the world through art were beginning to develop; new orders of beauty were beginning to emerge. Finally, if we look at a painting from the early Renaissance period as seen in Figure 2.3, we see an even more pronounced shift.

> **Aesthetics** is the branch of philosophy concerned with the study of beauty and taste. Because aesthetics is concerned with how judgements concerning the beautiful are made, it has a closeness to ethics which seeks to determine the good and/or moral.

The Birth of Venus, a tempera on canvas by Sandro Botticelli (*c.* 1484–1486) shifts the subject matter from religious scenes to the mythological. Moreover, though the scene rendered is clearly one of myth and fantasy, the figures in the painting appear to be much more detailed and realistic. There is also clear foreground and background, lending additional depth and perspective. Again, this is indicative of a shift towards new forms of beauty as portrayed in art. This may seem somewhat aside from social work being couched in **aesthetics**, yet of beauty, Howe (1994: 518) tells us that:

When social workers care, they are concerned about the quality of the other's experience. ... The connection between the ugliness of people's lives and the harmony of the social order is well recognized. If beauty and satisfying form are the outward expression of an object's inner state, then it behoves social workers to recognize the principles upon which beauty is based so that they can ensure that clients' lives can be lived aesthetically as well as justly and effectively.

This assertion from Howe (1994) allows us to think about beauty in more abstract terms as something that social workers are perhaps concerned with pursuing for the betterment of those they work with as a component of the pursuit of justice that changes or transforms ugliness to beauty.

Figure 2.1: *Madonna and Child*, possibly 1230s, a tempera on wood by Berlinghiero

Source: Heritage Images Partnership / Alamy

Figure 2.2: *Lamentation (The Mourning of Christ)* by Giotto Di Bondone, 1305

Source: Niday Picture Library / Alamy

Figure 2.3: *The Birth of Venus*, a tempera on canvas by Sandro Botticelli (*c.* 1484–1486)

Source: Adam Eastland / Alamy

Reformation

Church reformation beginning in the 16th century coincided with and was encapsulated within the Renaissance and was a significant feature of development and change as new forms of Christianity were being initiated. Led initially by **Martin Luther**, these new forms of Christianity questioned and problematised the existing relationship between people in general and the church. Luther's

> **Martin Luther** (10 November 1483 to 18 February 1546) was a German priest, theologian, author, hymnwriter, professor and Augustinian friar. He was the seminal figure of the Protestant Reformation, and his theological beliefs form the basis of Lutheranism.

argument was that 'salvation was within the gift of God and God alone: it could not be granted by any other; it could not be purchased by indulgence; and it was attainable only through faith in the Lord Jesus Christ and by living in accordance with the Christian fate' (Whelan, 2021: 41). These ideas, which were extremely radical at the time, were communicated through printing press technology that allowed them to proliferate widely. Luther's message was one of thrift and self-sacrifice and the Protestant Reformation changed the shape and practice of faith and of the faithful. This, as the sociologist **Max Weber** (1902/2001) most famously theorised, had major ramifications for capital acquisition and was one of a number of seeds that would eventually help to grow an emerging capitalism.

> **Max Weber** (21 April 1864 to 14 June 1920) was a German sociologist, historian and political economist. He is regarded as among the most important theorists of the development of modern western society. His ideas profoundly influence social theory and research.

Liberalism and democracy

A further area to consider with respect to unpacking the constituent parts of modernity is that of liberalism and democracy. As the Enlightenment progressed and people were beginning to be broadly seen as capable of reasoning and making decisions about their own lives, questions of governance and of how societies should be broadly organised began to surface. This was a time of increasing recognitions: recognitions that were made manifest through the development of rights and freedoms. A move away from church dominance was coupled with a move away from monarchy and the 'divine right of kings', to be replaced with a move towards constitutional democracy. In his famous essay on 'Citizenship and Social Class', **T.H. Marshall** (1950) set out the

> **T.H. Marshall** (19 December 1893 to 29 November 1981) was an English sociologist and is best known for his essay 'Citizenship and Social Class', a key work on citizenship that introduced the idea that full citizenship includes civil, political and social citizenship.

development of rights across three spectrums that included civil, political and social rights, noting that:

Civil rights are composed of:

> the rights necessary for individual freedom-liberty of the person, freedom of speech, thought and faith, the right to own property and to conclude valid contracts, and the right to justice. (Marshall, 1950: 10)

Political rights are composed of:

> the right to participate in the exercise of political power, as a member of a body invested with political authority or as an elector of the members of such a body. The corresponding institutions are parliament and councils of local government. (Marshall, 1950: 11)

And social rights are composed of:

> the whole range from the right to a modicum of economic welfare and security to the right to share to the full in the social heritage and to live the life of a civilised being according to the standards prevailing in the society. The institutions most closely connected with it are the educational system and the social services. (Marshall, 1950: 11)

Broadly speaking, for Marshall (1950), with many fits and starts, these rights developed from approximately the beginning of the 18th century to the early part of the 20th century. Civil and political rights happened first and coincided with or were broadly aligned with Enlightenment thinking. Social rights happened later and became most notably embedded through the development of post-war welfare states. Social work as an activity is clearly concerned with rights and most clearly concerned with the post-war social rights that make up a core component of modernity or the condition of being modern.

The Industrial Revolution

The final area of attention with respect to sketching out the constituent parts of what would form the basis of modernity is the Industrial Revolution. Beginning in Britain in approximately the mid-18th century and lasting until approximately the mid-19th century, the first Industrial Revolution gave rise to a series of changes that would have seismic repercussions lasting through to the present day. In the first instance, the Industrial Revolution gave rise to new forms of social life as cities grew in size and population and became industrial and manufacturing hubs, creating great wealth for some and giving rise to great poverty and hardship for others.

Social relationships based on capitalism are also firmly cemented during this time, which in turn gave rise to distinct social classes: some who would have to seek to sell their labour to survive and some who would seek to purchase that labour to realise profit. Globalisation begins to accelerate at this juncture, as trade across country borders also increases. This is also a very important juncture for social work, which in effect emerged out of a burgeoning capitalism as noted by Philp (1979) who argues that social work emerged as a form of 'governmentality' in conditions of industrialisation at the turn of the 19th century. 'Clients', Philp (1979) argued, were 'produced' in terms of their social potential as opposed to their social rights. Howe's (1994) later assertion that social work is effectively a 'child of modernity' resonates with this. Taking both Philp's (1979) and Howe's (1994) assertions together, social work might be seen as a peculiar symptom of modernity, having arisen through the distinct sets of social relations that persist through modernity.

Key characteristics

Many of the theorists who will be covered in this book will have sought to interrogate some aspect of modernity or, indeed, will have been working in the tradition of what might be broadly referred to as traditional modernity. Therefore, having now noted some of the key components of a developing modernity, it is worth finally noting some of the characteristics of modernity itself. As noted at the outset of this chapter, modernity is suggested to be radically different from all previous forms of social life. In this respect, key components to keep in mind are as follows:

- Capitalism
  - As opposed to primitive accumulation
- Mass production
  - As opposed to discrete production
- Urbanisation
  - Waning rural life
- Rise of the nation state
  - Liberalism as opposed to monarchy
- Western domination
  - Western ways of knowing
- Secular forms of knowledge and expertise
  - The birth of the expert

Social work and modernity

Howe (1994) describes social work as a 'child of modernity' and suggests that the three 'traditional cornerstones' of social work are *care, confront* and *control*. These components of social work will be immediately recognisable to anyone studying or practising in the discipline and have since been expanded on by other social work theorists (see Thompson, 2009). However, these key aspects of social work did not arise in a vacuum, and it is important to understand where they come from and what they are grounded in. To do this, Howe (1994: 518) aligns these cornerstones with what he describes as modernity's three great projects that aim to pursue the good, the beautiful and the true:

> In its own way, social work has pursued the beautiful (aesthetics), the good (ethics) and the true (science) as it attempts to bring about a pleasing quality of life and a just society by using the insights of the social sciences.

Taking Howe's (1994) description as a starting point, we have already noted that social work may be seen to pursue the beautiful, in the abstract at least, by pursuing better lives and conditions for those who encounter social work and who social work encounters. Sometimes this may require care, it may require confrontation and it may even require control. Similarly, modern social work clearly operates to a code of ethics that prescribes what social work holds to be good. Again, social workers pursue the good through caring, confronting and potentially controlling where necessary. The capacity to pursue the beautiful and the good via the mechanisms of care, confront and control come via a third of modernity's great projects in the form of the true. In other words, to have the capacity to practice social work legitimately and effectively, the profession must have a truth or series of truths at its core: truths that are based in rational, reasonable thought, truths that make claims about what is beautiful and what is moral and good, and these are accessed and attained through social work education. However, social work as a 'child of modernity' arguably now finds itself in a postmodern world where being confident about what is beautiful, what is good and what is true is far less certain.

Postmodernity

Where modernity as a project kept faith with the principles of the Enlightenment, postmodernity effectively tore up the playbook to suggest that there were no universal truths, that beauty was in the eye of the beholder and not subject to a universal standard and that the good was merely what people believed to be good in a given place and at a given time. As a phase or stage in human and social development the 'post' in postmodernity signifies that this is a stage beyond or 'after' modernity. Alongside being a stage beyond modernity, postmodernity is also a reaction to and indictment of modernity that is seen as failed project; a project that not only didn't deliver on the ideals of truth, beauty and the good but that has become dull, stagnant, aloof and even repressive. Clearly this is deeply problematic for social work as a 'child of modernity' that adheres to a universal and true vision of the beautiful, the good and the true. Smith (2011: 2–3) brings the uncertain nature of postmodernity into stark relief in the following terms:

Modernity seeks to impose order upon increasing uncertainty through ever-more elaborate systems to assess, monitor and manage risk. If modernity seeks order, postmodernity is governed by the will to individual happiness and a relinquishing of the regulatory impulse. The result of this, however, is anxiety, brought about by a sacrificing of modernity's promise of security. The world is experienced as overwhelmingly uncertain, uncontrollable and frightening.

What then can social work do in the face of a burgeoning postmodernity where even basic moral reasoning is questioned and problematised? This question will be answered further on. For now, however, some of the key factors of postmodernity are described.

Key factors of postmodernity

Deconstruction

Not unlike modernity, there is no universally agreed timeline for when societies entered a postmodern phase. Moreover, not everyone agrees that a distinct phase called postmodernity has ever really come into being. However, whatever side of the fence you sit on, there is widespread agreement that the philosophy of **Nietzsche** was formative

> **Friedrich Wilhelm Nietzsche** (15 October 1844 to 25 August 1900) was a German philosopher, prose poet, cultural critic, philologist and composer whose work has exerted a profound influence on contemporary philosophy.

to the ideas that shape what some people call postmodernity. Nietzsche continually challenged what might have been seen as orthodox or mainstream philosophy in his work. More than this, he sought to tear down or deconstruct all that had gone before. That he did so in a scathing and often humorous way ushered in hallmarks that have also come to characterise postmodernist art and thinking wherein humour and absurdity often feature. In his work *On the Genealogy of Morals* (1887/2008), Nietzsche argued that morality was historically contingent and that there was no universal moral code that was good for all times and all places. In this way, he took aim at the prospect of developing a set of universal ethics. However, Nietzsche refused to replace what he tore down and instead suggested that whosoever wills truth or morals or the good into being does, for a time at least, make it so. This tendency towards deconstruction without any attempt at reconstruction has characterised much of what is associated with postmodernity. This has meant that basic questions, perhaps once thought settled, are once again up for deconstruction and debate so that we might ask:

- What is beauty?
- What is order?

- What is knowledge?
- What is truth?
- What is real?
- What is moral?
- What is human nature?

> **Poststructuralism** refers to a way of thinking that emphasises that knowledge is uncertain and that 'truth' is not a fixed concept, but instead changes based on cultural, political and social contexts.

While the philosophy of Nietzsche was undoubtedly influential and Nietzsche may certainly be thought of as a canonical figure in the context of postmodernity, much of what would perhaps be most closely associated with postmodernity emerged in its strongest form in the 1970s onwards where, in the realm of social theory at least, it tended to get mixed up with **poststructuralism**. Postmodernism and poststructuralism both describe theoretical movements in the late 20th century, and both tend to be used interchangeably. As a rule, postmodernism as a movement, separate from postmodernity as a phase of human and social development, tends to be more associated with literature whereas poststructuralism is more associated with theory and philosophy. Key in both movements, however, is a tendency towards deconstruction.

Challenging truths

Howe (1994: 521) notes that:

> Those who detect a shift from the modern to the postmodern describe a number of features that characterize the postmodern condition. The most pervasive notion is that there are no transcendent, universal criteria of truth, judgement and taste that can be applied to all situations at all times in all places.

If the factors that ultimately constituted a phase in human and social development that has come to be known as modernity were those of great historical shifts and movements, the move towards postmodernity has arguably been more subtle and largely conceptual. Yet just as with the project of modernising, the shift towards the postmodern can be detected in things like art, architecture, music and literature. As noted earlier, postmodernity is as much a reaction against modernity as it is a stage beyond it and so much of the postmodern project devolves upon challenging what is seen as universally true in some way. To offer an analogy as to how truth can be challenged using literature, we might first ask the question: what would happen to what we know, what we feel and what we believe in a different world?

You might be tempted to say that what you know, feel and believe would remain the same as you would be unchanged. Turning our attention to a different world, albeit fictional, we can use the example of Anarres from *The Dispossessed* by **Ursula K. Le Guin** (1974) to tease this out further. The language spoken on Anarres, which is called Pravic, reflects the **anarchism** of that society. In turn, Pravic as a language reflects many aspects of the philosophical foundations of utopian anarchism. For instance, the use of the possessive case is strongly discouraged, being almost entirely absent. Children are trained to speak only about matters that interest others; anything else is 'egoising'. There is also no property ownership of any kind. If you grew up on Anarres speaking Pravic, would the things you know, feel and believe be the same as they are now? Would your universal truths still hold true? If the answer is 'no' or if you have doubts, what does this tell us about the universality of truth?

> **Ursula K. Le Guin** (21 October 1929 to 22 January 2018) was an American author best known for her works of speculative fiction, including science fiction works set in her Hainish universe, and the Earthsea fantasy series.

A further way to understand how the thought associated with postmodernity challenges truth and convention is to once again turn our attention to artistic forms and the philosophy of aesthetics. Postmodernist art, as it appeared in the 1970s, is often loosely connected to the poststructural philosophical movement. Thematically, there is little to unite postmodern art in the way that other movements or periods are united other than the idea perhaps that anything goes. The use of unusual materials and of mechanical processes also tends to feature and humour is also often employed. Conceptually, postmodern art

> **Anarchism** is a political philosophy and movement that is sceptical of all justifications for authority and seeks to abolish them, including governments, nation states and capitalism. Anarchism advocates for the replacement of the state with stateless societies and voluntary free associations.

and postmodern artists suggested that the meaning behind or the very act of making the art can be more important than the art itself. In the context of challenging modernity's truths, there was also the belief that anything could be used to make art, that art could take any form and that there should be no differentiation between high art and low art. As an example of postmodernist art, *The Physical Impossibility of Death in the Mind of Someone Living* is an artwork created in 1991 by Damien Hirst that consists of a preserved tiger shark submerged in formaldehyde in a glass–panel display case (see Figure 2.4).

This striking piece of art is very different to classical or traditional art of any period. Defying convention, it is peculiarly modern and arguably challenges all that has come before. In this way, we can suggest that it defies modernity's truths in the context of what might have traditionally come to be known as beautiful or good. Is this an example of 'good' art? Is it beautiful? Who gets to decide?

Figure 2.4: *The Physical Impossibility of Death in the Mind of Someone Living,* an artwork created in 1991 by Damien Hirst

Source: El Chapulin / Alamy

Key characteristics

Having given a brief overview of what makes postmodernity different and distinct from modernity, it is worth further noting some of the key characteristics of postmodernity. As noted earlier, postmodernity is not only a stage beyond modernity but also a reaction to and against modernity. In this respect, key components to keep in mind are as follows:

- A rejection of any universal ideas about things like truth, knowledge, beauty or human nature.
- A tendency towards deconstruction of existing ways of knowing.
- The admission of multiple ways of knowing.

Social work and postmodernity

On the surface, postmodernity as a phase of human and social development and as a reaction to and against the project of modernity can seem troubling for social work. Atherton and Bolland (2002: 431) reflect this by suggesting that postmodernism represents a dangerous illusion for social work. They argue that:

> Social workers cannot be postmodernists because they operate from a set
> of convictions that they believe are qualitatively better than competing
> sets. While there may be no eternal, absolute, unchanging truths and

understandings in the sense that our medieval forbears thought of such things, there can be standards for best practice or best policy, subject to empirical evidence and critical review.

Atherton and Bolland (2002) are firm here: social work is not a space for 'anything goes' and social workers need to wary of the allure of postmodernity and keep faith with modernity's truths, which are based on evidence and critical review. Yet perhaps something can be retrieved for social work from postmodern perspectives; perhaps deconstruction in particular can lead to forms of good social work practice. If we were to suggest that deconstruction challenges taken-for-granted theories and ideas in social work including expert opinions and the use of power to shape knowledge, we might next be able to suggest that no one has a monopoly of truth. In practice, this could mean hearing everyone's voice, fostering inclusion and negotiation, paying attention to differing social contexts and to how meaning changes in these contexts. This, in turn, could also lead us to ask why some forms of knowledge are valued over others and to challenge assessment judgements that put service users into boxes and instead value difference. In this respect, being prepared to admit some of the factors that characterise postmodernity into social work practice could encourage pluralism with respect to knowledge as well as participation and partnership.

Summary

This chapter has introduced modernity and postmodernity. We have seen that modernity as a phase in human and social development has been shaped and formed by many things including the Enlightenment, the Reformation, the Industrial Revolution and a move towards rights and liberal democracy. Drawing on Howe (1994), we have seen that modernity as a project is characterised by the good, the beautiful and the true and that these manifest in social work through care, confront and control. We have also seen a challenge to modernity's truths through the advent of postmodernity as a reaction to and against modernity. In postmodernity, we find the very notion of truth challenged. Moreover, we find that universal ideas about beauty and morality are challenged and problematised. Yet we also find the potential for a social work practice that values multiple ways of knowing and so can be inclusive. In the chapters to follow, each of the theorists who are covered will be located broadly in either traditional modernity or postmodernity. Therefore, you should be able to take what has been covered here and use it to add an additional layer of understanding to your learning.

For students: Exercise box 2

In this chapter we spent some time focusing on the differences between traditional modernity and postmodernity. This exercise will help you to interrogate your understanding:

1. Focusing on what you read in this chapter, think about the differences between modernity and postmodernity. What do you understand these to be? Write these down.
2. Now think about social work. What are social work's truths under modernity? How does postmodern thought challenge these?

Further reading
- Referred to several times during the chapter, David Howe's classic essay on 'Modernity, postmodernity and social work' is well worth a read.
- Howe, D. (1994) 'Modernity, postmodernity and social work', *British Journal of Social Work*, 24: 513–32.
- Mentioned at the end of the previous chapter, the following book by Paul Michael Garrett covers similar themes and will help to further deepen your understanding:
- Garrett, P.M. (2018) *Social Work and Social Theory – Making Connections*, Bristol: Policy Press.

Why not watch!
There are many useful clips on YouTube that may help to flesh out and deepen your understanding. One that is particularly useful is called 'Modernism vs. postmodernism', which is published by The Living Philosophy YouTube channel and can be found at: https://youtu.be/iMVjI3pcwcU

Chapter references
Atherton, C.R. and Bolland, K.A. (2002) 'Postmodernism: a dangerous illusion for social work', *International Social Work*, 45(4): 421–33.

Foucault, M. (1966/2002) *The Order of Things: An Archaeology of the Human Sciences*, London: Routledge.

Howe, D. (1994) 'Modernity, postmodernity and social work', *British Journal of Social Work*, 24: 513–32.

Kuhn, T.S. (1962) *The Structure of Scientific Revolutions*, Chicago: University of Chicago Press.

Le Guin, U.K. (1974) *The Dispossessed*, New York: Harper Voyager.

Marshall, T.H. (1950) *Citizenship and Social Class and Other Essays*, London: Cambridge University Press.

Nietzsche, F. (1887/2008) *On the Genealogy of Morals*, Oxford: Oxford University Press.

Philp, M. (1979) 'Notes on the form of knowledge in social work', *Sociological Review*, 27(1): 83–111.

Smith, M. (2011) 'Reading Bauman for social work', *Ethics and Social Welfare*, 5(1): 2–17.

Thompson, N. (2009) *Understanding Social Work*, Basingstoke: Palgrave Macmillan.

Weber, M. (1902/2001) *The Protestant Ethic and the Spirit of Capitalism*, Abingdon: Routledge.

Whelan, J. (2021) *Welfare, Deservingness and the Logic of Poverty: Who Deserves?* Newcastle upon Tyne: Cambridge Scholars Publishing.

For instructors: A set of slides that accompany this chapter can be accessed through the book webpage at: https://policy.bristoluniversitypress.co.uk/critical-theory-for-social-work.

3

Karl Marx and social work

Biographical note

Karl Marx was born in Trier, Germany, on 5 May 1818. Marx studied law and philosophy at the universities of Bonn, Berlin and later Jenna where he was awarded a doctorate. His intellectual life was characterised by a long-standing partnership with his friend, collaborator and sometime financial backer, Friedrich Engels, with whom he wrote *The Communist Manifesto* and other works. A controversial and influential figure in his own lifetime, Marx spent much of his life in exile. After being expelled from Germany, Marx moved to London in 1849, where he lived for the rest of his life. He died impoverished on 14 March 1883 (aged 64) in London and is buried in the Tomb of Karl Marx in Highgate Cemetery. Key texts by Marx include *The Economic and Philosophic Manuscripts of 1844* (1844/2007), *The Communist Manifesto* (1848/1992), written with Friedrich Engels, and his magnum opus *Das Kapital* (1867/2013).

Introduction

Few people have had as utterly profound an effect on the world as Karl Marx and there are many reasons to include Marx's work in a book on critical social theory. In the first instance, Marx can rightly be thought of as the quintessential critical theorist and though his project was in some ways one of critique and deconstruction, overall, his work is most comfortably located in traditional modernity as Marx (1867/2013, np) sought ultimately 'to lay bare the economic law of motion of modern society'. A political philosopher to some, an economist to others and a canonical figure in sociology, Marx was also an activist, an organiser and a revolutionary figure. Marx's output over the various stages of his writing career was reasonably prolific. Yet it pales in comparison to the amount of work that has been written by others since about Marx's intellectual contributions (Whelan 2021). This rich corpus of material, written both by Marx himself and by others, including many social work theorists, offers a range of conceptual and theoretical tools that can be useful when thinking about social work. Garrett (2018: 179) affirms this by noting that 'Marx continues to furnish analytical "reminders" or "coordinates" to understand the present'. This relevance and usefulness is also noted by Lavalette (2020: 19) who suggests that:

> while there isn't a 'Marxist social work', Marx's work provides us with a powerful set of ideas that help us understand the contemporary world of competitive, global capitalism and the myriad problems such a system creates.

With this in mind, the following core Marxist concepts will be introduced, described and related to social work:

- The Marxist dialectic.
- Marx's perspective on social class and the capitalist mode of production.
- Species being and alienation.

The chapter will finish with a short summary and, as with previous chapters, some exercises and further materials will be flagged at the end of the chapter. In keeping with the goal for this book, the concepts explored here, which are complex and often contested, will be introduced in simple terms while encouraging the interested reader to use the materials provided to go further and deepen understanding.

The Marxist dialectic

Marx was not the first philosopher to use the idea of the dialectic as a form of reasoning. However, he did arguably take it in a new direction. Classically, dialectic is a form of reasoning based upon dialogue, argument and counterargument that moves the parties involved towards agreement. In developing his own mode of dialectic, Marx was particularly influenced by what has become known as the 'Hegelian dialectic', a form of dialectic reasoning attributed to Georg Wilhelm Friedrich **Hegel**. The Hegelian dialectic is a three-stage dialectic that starts with a thesis, the reaction or counterargument to this thesis forms an antithesis and the differences between the two are ultimately resolved by means of a synthesis that effectively represents a higher order of thought and allows the parties involved to move forward. This version of the dialectic is positively oriented and, for Hegel, operates at a level far above individual disputes and dialogue and is representative of the way societies progress towards truth and towards 'higher thought' generally. In reality, the 'Hegelian dialectic' has to be read into Hegel's work as he never used the thesis, antithesis, synthesis formula and was in many ways inspired by the work of Immanuel **Kant**. Nevertheless, Marx was

> **Georg Wilhelm Friedrich Hegel** (27 August 1770 to 14 November 1831) was a German philosopher and one of the most influential figures of 19th-century philosophy. He had a huge influence on the early thought of Karl Marx, who briefly associated with a group known as the 'Young Hegelians' before eventually breaking with Hegelian ideas.

> Born in Königsberg, Germany, **Immanuel Kant** (22 April 1724 to 12 February 1804) was a German philosopher and a central figure of the Enlightenment. He is widely regarded as one of the most influential figures in modern western philosophy and his work on ethics has been influential in the context of social work.

undoubtedly inspired by Hegel and his own version of the dialectic holds many similarities in form if not in content. The starting point for Marx's dialectic is to suggest that human nature is not predetermined or universal and stands in a direct relationship with society. For Marx, human nature arises as a result of a dialectical relationship between persons and the society they inhabit, each affecting, shaping and influencing the other (Whelan, 2021). Even though human nature for Marx was formed and shaped through what was close at hand as given by preceding generations, in general it remained open and changeable, meaning that there was always potential for self-determination and new forms of freedom (Lavalette, 2020). Distilling this down further, however, it is the contradictions within societies that were key for Marx. These contradictions include things like the contradictions that occur through social class or that are characterised by labour economics, the contradictions at the heart of capitalistic social relations and the socioeconomic interactions that this creates. For Marx, such contradictions effectively form the engine that drives society forward. However, unlike the Hegelian dialectic wherein higher truths, ideas and forms of progress are arrived at through thesis, antithesis and synthesis, for Marx the contradictions at the core of modern societies are rooted in material conditions that lead to progress for some and deterioration for others. Bearing this out, Vickers (2019), notes that Marxism directs attention to the way consciousness is shaped by experience, and how experience is shaped in turn by social structures, in particular the processes of production and reproduction.

Thinking about social work

When thinking about the Marxist dialectic in the context of social work, it is perhaps best used to think about how social work has developed over time. Social work as a profession is riven with tensions, contradictory positions and dichotomies through which it has developed (Whelan 2022). Care versus control, pursuing social justice versus maintaining social order, grassroots activist social work versus professionalised and proceduralised social work: studying the history of these contradictory positions can help us to understand how social work has come to be the profession it is today. In this way, we can use the Marxist dialectic to interrogate and understand much about social work. The Marxist dialectic can also be used to think about the contradictions that exist in wider society that are rooted in material conditions. In turn, this can help social workers to think about the contradictions that can characterise service users' lives.

Marx's perspective on social class and the capitalist mode of production

The contradictions and conflict that arose through societies being stratified along class lines, was, for Marx and for Engels, the engine that drove and shaped history. This they summed up most famously in *The Communist Manifesto* (1848/1992: 4) in the following terms:

The history of all hitherto existing society is the history of class struggle. Freeman and slave, patrician and plebeian, lord and serf, guild master and journeyman, in a word, oppressor and oppressed, stood in constant opposition to one another, carried on an uninterrupted, now hidden, now open fight, a fight that each time ended, either in a revolutionary reconstitution of society at large or in the common ruin of contending classes.

> In Marxist theory, the **economic base** refers to the forces of production including the materials and resources that generate the goods needed by society. The **superstructure** describes all other aspects of society not directly related to production including things like art, the law, politics, education. These effectively 'sit upon' the economic base.

> **Commodities**, simply defined, are all goods and services that can be bought or sold in a marketplace. This includes everything from luxury goods to raw materials needed in production to care services. Under the Marxist theory of political economy, the labour of persons is also a commodity that can be bought and sold.

Dialectic reasoning is again apparent here and, for Marx and Engels, it is the contradictions and oppositions between class groups that gives texture to history. In the contemporary sense, for Marx, class was about the tensions and relationships that existed under the capitalist mode of production that was burgeoning in his lifetime, creating great wealth for some and poverty and immiseration for others. Marx theorised that production was the engine that drove class relations and gave rise to society so that society consisted of an **economic base and social superstructure**. Class struggle under capitalism was a struggle that was predominantly being fought between two groups: the workers 'the working class or the *proletariat*', who had to sell their labour in order to reproduce themselves; and the owners of the means of production 'the bourgeoise', who purchased and used that labour to produce **commodities** that could then be brought to market for sale and the realisation of profit. On commodities, Marx (1867/2013: 10) noted that:

The wealth of all those societies in which the capitalist mode of production prevails, presents itself as an immense accumulation of commodities.

The production of commodities is therefore key to the capitalist cycle and the accumulation of wealth. Those who owned the means of production, things like land, property, machinery and raw materials, were possessed of almost all the ingredients needed to produce commodities with the exception being labour. This, however, could be treated like a commodity and purchased through the offer of wages. However, while this might seem like a reasonable arrangement, Marx drew attention to the fact that in reality it was a deeply unequal one and replete with elements of power, coercion and exploitation. On the one hand, the capitalist's singular purpose is the realisation of profit. Moreover, under the capitalist mode of production Marx suggested that the capitalist was compelled to do everything possible to realise a profit because of coercive competition, which would effectively drive less profitable operations out of business. On the other hand, the worker wishes to reproduce him/herself by selling the only commodity at his/her disposal: his/her labour for wages. Both parties have a right to realise the best conditions possible for themselves. However, Marx noted that between equal rights, force ultimately decides. The labourer will often have no choice but to submit to the conditions on offer in order to have some chance at reproducing themselves and their dependents. Marx (1867/2013: 451) summed up this exploitative relationship by noting that the:

> socially productive power of labour develops as a free gift to capital whenever the workers are placed under certain conditions, and it is capital which places them under these conditions.

These conditions often included a choice between pauperism or long hours, dangerous and dirty work and insufficient renumeration. In time, trade unions would seek to level the playing field for workers and many concessions around working conditions were won. However, the relationship between workers and the owners of the means of production would still be seen by Marx as inherently exploitative, alienating and very much in favour of the capitalist class.

Thinking about social work

So, how can the Marxist conception of social class and the capitalist mode of production be useful tools for thinking about social work? In the first instance, we can think about where social work as an occupation sits within capitalist societies and what its relationship is to the mode of production. We can also think about where social workers as workers fit within this. In this respect, Knickmeyer (1972: 63) notes that 'the human service worker is in an important position to effect change – even if he [sic] is somewhat peripheral to the means of production'. Taking the second part of this assertion by Knickmeyer (1972) forward, we might begin by saying that social work sits within the superstructure, having little to do directly with the economic base. Yet, Knickmeyer was writing in 1972 and since then there has been an ongoing process of commodification in the areas of health and human services, meaning that what social workers 'produce' now in the form of a service has begun to take on the character of a commodity, something that can be bought and sold in the market. This, in turn is reflective of the general commodification of social life and aspects of the life course. This may mean that social workers have, perhaps unwittingly, begun to form part of the economic base to some degree. Certainly, the concerns of the social worker as a worker are often the same concerns as any other worker, namely decent pay and conditions. The social worker as worker then has some common ground with the traditional working class. Yet, despite creeping commodification, social work remains a peculiarly bourgeois profession (Whelan, 2022) and so if we return to the first part of Knickmeyer's (1972) assertion, this notes that social workers may be uniquely placed to effect change. This, in turn, allows us to return to the concept of class in terms of who social workers are likely to seek to help and affect change with and for. In this respect, from its beginnings as a charitable endeavour, social work has always had a large presence in working-class, poor and disadvantaged communities. From this perspective, using a Marxist analysis of class to help understand the broader challenges that working-class and disadvantaged communities can face can help to strengthen social work practice and assessment by moving beyond individualising perspectives to incorporate a more fulsome analysis.

Alienation

The final area of Marxist theory to be covered in this chapter is that of alienation. Alienation is a popular and well-known Marxist concept. However, it must also be noted that alienation represents a concept from the earlier period in what many people see as two distinct phases in Marx's career. Early work by Marx (1844/2007) suggested that the capitalist mode of production gave rise to a rift in species being, that is, the exploitation of the working classes by the capitalist classes had the effect of moving human beings away from how they would naturally and preferably exist in the world. Marx situates concepts like species being within the broader concept of alienation, something that he later advanced considerably in the *Grundrisse* (1857–58/1993). Still influenced by Hegel, the Marx who wrote about alienation is argued by some to be a purely philosophical or ideological Marx communicating about purely philosophical ideas. In later work and in *Das Kapital* (1867/2013) in particular, Marx sought to advance his ideas as a science that went beyond the speculative philosophy of Hegel and other of his influences, and so alienation as a term falls out of use. This young/old–philosophical/scientific 'phases of Marx' thesis was most famously represented by the French Marxist intellectual Louis Althusser, who referred to a move towards a more scientific analysis in his work as Marx's 'epistemological break'. Whether the 'epistemological break' thesis holds or not, we will take the concept of alienation at face value and note that though perhaps it is not mentioned directly, there is much in Marx's later work that speaks to alienation in a practical sense still.

Like so much of what he theorised, Marx of course locates his ideas about alienation in the relationships formed between persons under the capitalist mode of production and in class relationships in particular, suggesting that these gave rise to a process of alienation. It should be noted that Marx has no issue with work as a 'thing in itself'. Work and using one's labour-power in a free and consenting manner is acknowledged by Marx as an inherent and fully natural part of what it means to be human (Whelan, 2021). However, things become much more complex when the labour-power of one set or group of persons is acquired by another group in return for wages. This essentially has the effect of inherently dehumanising the worker by alienating them from what they have produced and rendering them, in effect, an 'appendage of the machine'. In *The Economic and Philosophic Manuscripts of 1844* (1844/2007: 70), Marx gives an account of alienation through the productive process in the following terms:

> The worker puts his life into the object; but now his life no longer belongs to him but to the object ... The alienation of the worker in his product means not only that his labour becomes an object, an external existence, but that it exists outside him, independently, as something alien to him, and that it becomes a power on its own confronting him; it means that the life which he has conferred on the object confronts him as something hostile and alien.

In this scenario, labour-power is purchased as just another commodity in the production process in order to generate surplus value for capitalist employers. The worker's life in the form of labour becomes congealed within an object over which he or she has no ownership. Not only this, but the object also becomes alien and hostile to the worker. Through this process of alienation, a process based in an exploitative relationship, the worker:

> does not affirm himself but denies himself, does not feel content but unhappy, does not develop freely his physical and mental energies but mortifies his body and ruins his mind. (*The Economic and Philosophic Manuscripts of 1844*: 72)

For Marx, alienation is four-dimensional, and the worker is separated from his or her product, from his or her labour, from himself or herself and, resultingly, from others.

Moving forward to his later work, in *Das Kapital* (1867/2013: 183) Marx gives practical expression to alienation through the capitalist mode of production in the following terms:

> the labourer is nothing else his whole life than labour ... therefore all his disposable time is by nature and law, labour-time, to be devoted to the self-expansion of capital. Time for education, for intellectual development, for the fulfilling of social functions and for social intercourse, for the free play of his bodily and mental activity, even the rest time of a Sunday.

This amounts to a devastating critique of capitalism and the capitalist mode of production, a mode of production under which human beings are alienated from many of the things that make them human and so remain in large part unfulfilled. This alienated form of life becomes a life that is essentially meaningless for persons who, having lost the capacity for self-determination have become 'unfree'. This in turn represents one of the great paradoxes of capitalism in liberal democracies: capitalism is often held up as being the only economic system that can ensure freedom. In fact, Nobel prize winning economists like Friedrich Hayek and Milton Friedman have argued strongly that this is the case. In *The Road to Serfdom*, Hayek (1944) argued against what he saw as the danger of a tyranny that could come from a move towards planned economies with strong welfare states, arguing that this would lead to a loss of the individualism that was couched in the liberal traditions and inevitably lead to a loss of freedom. In *Capitalism and Freedom*, Friedman (1962) essentially argues that economic freedom forms a prerequisite to the political freedoms associated with the Enlightenment. In both visions a more or less unfettered capitalism is seen as essential to freedom and moreover, is seen as being good for both workers and employers who can bargain and who can each seek to realise their terms in a competitive marketplace. Yet, this belies the fact that people effectively sell their labour out of an inherent need to do so and as an aspect of survival, more or less good depending on what their skillset allows them to realise in terms of pay and conditions. So then, workers enter into this relationship not because of the freedoms afforded to them by capitalism, or at least not fully so, but rather as an aspect of necessity. Of necessity and freedom, Marx, in *Das Kapital* (1867/2013: 593) suggests that:

> the realm of freedom actually begins only where labour which is determined by necessity and mundane considerations ceases; thus in the very nature of things it lies beyond the sphere of actual material production.

Marx's conception of freedom is very different to freedom under the capitalist mode of production, and it is also arguably a much more humane vision. It is a type of freedom wherein people are not forced to sell their labour as an aspect of survival. It is a freedom then in which the necessities of persons are met and therefore the need to enter into an alienating labour process is rendered moot.

Yet for Marx, and for those who have built upon Marx's theory of alienation, it is not confined solely to the labour process. Rather, in yet another contradiction inherent in capitalism, employment through which to become alienated is not even guaranteed. Capitalism alienates whole swathes of people by reckoning their value through what they can or can't contribute to the market. Skills flit from useful to meaningless seemingly overnight, businesses close and **whole industries go out of business**, those who cannot work due to youth, old age, injury, illness, caring

> **Deindustrialisation** serves as a stark example of widespread alienation as industries such as the coal industry close down, leaving hundreds in affected communities unemployed and bereft of identity. Deindustrialised spaces across the UK, Europe and United States are continually linked with feelings of alienation and loss of belonging. Moreover, health and social problems have tended to rise steeply in former industrial zones. See Scheiring and King (2023) for an excellent life history study based in Hungary.

responsibilities, disability or other devalued characteristics are rendered valueless. There are also too many people and not enough jobs, creating an effective **reserve army of labour** who may be forced to take low-paid, precarious employment, for which they often have to compete; that is, if they find employment at all. Any of these circumstances can contribute to experiences of alienation in a society that is organised to extract surplus value from all possible quarters while rendering all else

> **Reserve army of labour** is a Marxist term used to describe the unemployed who often through the absence of any meaningful choice are prepared to work for very low wages in temporary jobs. The existence of a reserve army of labour serves the interests of the capitalist class and exploits members of the working class.

valueless. Effectively, life under the capitalist mode of production breeds these kinds of harsh and uncaring conditions. Such conditions are alienating in and of themselves, yet they are doubly alienating in that they foster practices and behaviours that Marx would argue were alien to human nature. Thus, we become alienated from ourselves, from our basic humanity and ultimately from each other.

Thinking about social work

C. Wright Mills (1963: 35): has noted that:

> The work of Marx taken as a whole is a savage sustained indictment of one alleged injustice; that the profit, the comfort, the luxury of one man is paid for by the loss, the misery, the denial of another.

In thinking about social work and Marx's conception of alienation, we can ask the question, 'What can alienation do?' and we can relate our answer to a number of key areas. If we first think about the social work value base, we can suggest that alienation under the capitalist mode of production as described by Marx limits the possibilities for client self-determination, not just in the social worker/service user relationship but in general. This means that social workers are often meeting individuals who may be limited in their freedoms and who may have limited control over many aspects of their lives. Moreover, social workers will often meet people who may feel alienated, dissatisfied or unfulfilled. Thinking back to the class analysis presented earlier in the chapter, social workers are also very likely to come into contact with poor, working-class and disadvantaged communities. These communities may have experienced significant alienation and stigmatisation. Within these communities and others, social workers may come into contact with people who have been alienated through the value judgements at the core of the capitalist mode of production and this includes unemployed people, older persons, persons with disabilities and many more. Finally, it is also worth noting that where individuals or whole communities are or become alienated, the kinds of social problems that social workers often encounter are much more likely to occur. Bearing this out, Ferguson and Lavalette (2004) have written about how aspects of alienation can drive the divisions that come to characterise many deeply entrenched social problems including racism, sexism and homophobia. Suffice to say that alienation as given by Marx is a powerful and illustrative concept and powerful analytical tool for social workers.

Summary

This chapter explored the theory of Karl Marx and demonstrated how it might be useful when thinking about social work. Use of the Marxist dialectic as tool for reasoning was introduced and it was shown that Marx saw the world as being internally contradictory and in a continuous process of change and flux. This, for Marx, was what drove the engine of history and so understanding this could allow for a greater understanding of society and its constituent parts. From there we explored Marx's theory of social class and the capitalist mode of production. We saw that for both Marx and Engels, class struggle had long characterised history in different forms and continued to characterise it in their own time as the working class entered into a struggle with the owners of the means of production. This struggle played out in the capitalist mode of production under which the worker wishes to adequately realise the pay and conditions needed to reproduce themselves and the capitalist sought to maximise profit. This, it was suggested, constituted an unequal playing field on which the power of the capitalist class was likely to win out. Finally, we looked at the Marxist theory of alienation and at how this is produced firstly through the labour process and more broadly through the way in which societies are constituted under capitalism. We saw how the effects of alienation on persons and communities were likely to be something that social workers encountered in their work. While much of what Marx presented is clearly couched in critique and it can be easy, therefore, to read his indictment of social relations as he found them and as we continue to find them through a veil of pessimism, it is worth remembering that Marx, as the foundational critical theorist, was concerned with revealing the conditions wrought by such social relations with a view to challenging and changing them. Indeed, within the broad corpus of their project, Marx and Engels speculate about a future beyond exploitative capitalism wherein people could hope to aspire to self-fulfilment, being free to 'hunt in the morning, fish in the afternoon, rear cattle in the evening and criticise after dinner' (*The German Ideology*, 1846/2007, p 54). Marx, therefore, alongside being a critic, should also be thought of as an emancipatory theorist whose vision of freedom and hope for the potential of humanity chime with the critical and radical foundations of emancipatory social work.

For students: Exercise box 3

In this chapter we explored the work of Karl Marx. To further explore your understanding, consider the following:

1. Use the dialectic method to think about the contradictions that have shaped social work. What are some of these?
2. Think about Marx's conception of class. How does it fit with today's world?
3. Think about some of the service users that social workers encounter. Could alienation be part of the reason they require social work intervention?

Further reading
-   If you would like to read something written by Marx himself, *The Communist Manifesto* is short, accessible and contains many of his key ideas.
-   Marx, K. and Engels, F. (1848/1992) *The Communist Manifesto*, Oxford: Oxford University Press.
-   This short chapter by Michael Lavalette is excellent and will lead you to many more interesting readings. Lavalette's work on Marx and social work is excellent in general.
-   Lavalette, M. (2020) 'Karl Marx: Capitalism, alienation and social work', in C. Morley, P. Ablett, P. Noble and S. Cowden (eds) *The Routledge Handbook of Critical Pedagogies for Social Work*, London: Routledge, pp 19–31.

Why not watch!
There are many useful clips on YouTube that may help to flesh out and deepen your understanding. One that is particularly useful is called 'Political theory – Karl Marx' and is published by The School of Life YouTube channel and available at: https://youtu.be/fSQgCy_iIcc

Why not listen!
Podcasts are a great way to learn! The following podcast is part of the BBC Sounds 'In Our Time' series. Marx as a person and a theorist is covered by leading experts. It is available here: https://www.bbc.co.uk/programmes/p003k9jg

Chapter references
Ferguson, I. and Lavalette, M. (2004) 'Beyond power discourse: alienation and social work', *British Journal of Social Work*, 34: 297–312.

Friedman, M. (1962) *Capitalism and Freedom*, Chicago: University of Chicago Press.

Garrett, P.M. (2018) 'Social work and Marxism: a short essay on the 200th anniversary of the birth of Karl Marx', *Critical and Radical Social Work*, 6(2): 179–96.

Hayek, F.A. (1944) *The Road to Serfdom*, London: Unwin Hyman.

Knickmeyer, R. (1972) 'A Marxist approach to social work', *Social Work*, 17(4): 58–65.

Lavalette, M. (2020) 'Karl Marx: Capitalism, alienation and social work', in C. Morley, P. Ablett, P. Noble and S. Cowden (eds) *The Routledge Handbook of Critical Pedagogies for Social Work*, London: Routledge, pp 19–31.

Marx, K. (1844/2007) *The Economic and Philosophic Manuscripts of 1844*, Mineola: Dover.

Marx, K. (1857–58/1993) *Grundrisse*, Harmondsworth: Penguin.

Marx, K. (1867/2013) *Das Kapital*, Hertfordshire: Wordsworth.

Marx, K. and Engels, F. (1848/1992) *The Communist Manifesto*, Oxford: Oxford University Press.

Scheiring, G. and King, L. (2023) 'Deindustrialization, social disintegration, and health: a neoclassical sociological approach', *Theory and Society*, 52: 145–78.

Vickers, T. (2019) 'Marxist social work', in S. Webb (ed) *The Routledge Handbook of Critical Social Work*, London: Routledge, pp 24–34.

Whelan, J. (2021) *Welfare, Deservingness and the Logic of Poverty: Who Deserves?* Newcastle upon Tyne: Cambridge Scholars Publishing.

Whelan, J. (2022). 'On your Marx…? A world to win or the dismantlement of a profession? On why we need a reckoning', *The British Journal of Social Work*, 52(2): 1168–81.

Wright Mills, C. (1963) *The Marxists*. Harmondsworth: Penguin.

For instructors: A set of slides that accompany this chapter can be accessed through the book webpage: https://policy.bristoluniversitypress.co.uk/critical-theory-for-social-work.

4

W.E.B. Du Bois and social work

Biographical note

William Edward Burghardt Du Bois, usually referred to as W.E.B. Du Bois was born on 23 February 1868, in Great Barrington, Massachusetts. Du Bois was an American sociologist, social historian and Pan-Africanist civil rights activist. As a theorist and a scholar, Du Bois lived and breathed what he wrote and was very much an activist and a campaigner through his written work. First attending the historically Black Fisk University in Nashville, Tennessee, Du Bois would go on to become the first African-American to be awarded a doctorate from Harvard University. Interestingly, and indicative of the deeply segregated world in which Du Bois found himself while also foreshadowing many of the themes he would grapple with as a sociologist, Du Bois first had to retake an undergraduate degree at Harvard before being able to progress towards doctoral study. This was because degrees from historically Black colleges and universities were not recognised by Harvard at that time. During his doctorate, Du Bois also undertook a scholarship in Berlin where he studied with and met many prominent social scientists of the time, including Max Weber. After completing his doctorate, Du Bois started his career as an academic in Wilberforce University in Ohio before taking up a post as a research assistant at the University of Pennsylvania in Philadelphia, the outcome of which would see the publication of his seminal study *The Philadelphia Negro* in 1899. This was an extraordinary piece of sociological research which was, unfortunately and to the detriment of the discipline, ignored by mainstream academia as were many of Du Bois's later contributions. Du Bois would subsequently go on to publish much more polemical work on many aspects of race and race relations. As an activist, Du Bois was one of the founders of the National Association for the Advancement of Colored People (NAACP), leaving the academy to work as a publicist and researcher for the same organisation. Indeed, as a sociologist and social theorist beyond the academy, Du Bois is particularly interesting from a social work perspective in that as a public intellectual he collaborated with some of the canonical figures in social work including with the women of Hull House, particularly Jane Addams and Florence Kelly, with whom he shared research concerns. Moreover, through the co-founding of the NAACP, Du Bois also cooperated with anti-racist social workers Mary White Ovington and Henry Moskowitz. Part of Du Bois's contribution therefore speaks directly to a less narrowly conceived, much more radical social work. Du Bois continued to publish during this time and spent the last years of his life in Ghana where he died in Accra on 27 August 1963 and was given a state funeral. *The Souls of Black Folk* (1903), the work that will be primarily drawn upon for this chapter, is undoubtedly one of Du Bois's most well-known and most notable works. *Black Reconstruction* (1935) is also considered by many to be Du Bois's magnum opus. However, taken together, his earlier empirical sociological work along with his later more polemic commentary represents a rich corpus of material that is testament to the prolific contribution of Du Bois across his lifetime. As a thinker in and doer of sociology in the traditional sense, Du Bois can be thought of as being associated with traditional modernity.

Introduction

In recent years, the work of W.E.B. Du Bois has begun to be reappraised as a part of a broad movement towards decolonising curricula and knowledge in general. While Du Bois may never really have been in danger of being fully 'lost to sociology', he was nevertheless thought of as somewhat of a minor figure and will arguably not have featured on very many introductory sociology courses as a founding figure of the discipline, though he almost certainly ought to have. There are many reasons for this, and they are not at all incidental or coincidental, rather they reflect the still deeply racially stratified America in which Du Bois lived and worked for most of his life. On the one hand, Du Bois was continuously professionally stymied and limited due to the colour of his skin. For example, he was limited to academic positions at historically Black universities which, while excellent institutions in their own right, routinely existed outside of mainstream academia. In his early career, when he did take up a position to undertake research at the University of Pennsylvania, a mainstream university attended by White students, he was given the title of 'sometime assistant in sociology' a contrived post which deliberately included no office or teaching responsibilities despite his holding a PhD from Harvard (Lewis, 1993). Yet, out of the research conducted during his time at the University of Pennsylvania Du Bois produced *The Philadelphia Negro* (1899), a study which has more recently, and rightly, been reappraised as the first American sociological study which looked at a specific group in detail (Anderson and Massey, 2001). However, if Du Bois had been stymied on a personal level, his work, despite the rigour and excellent nature of the sociological insights on offer, suffered a similar fate through being at one point almost written out of history. When one returns to *The Philadelphia Negro* (1899) now, it is clear that this historical omission is one that hurt sociology as a discipline by failing to recognise the work as an early example of what could be described as sociology as 'muckraking' or critical sociology. Muckraking in the sociological sense can be associated with the work of social reformer and photographer, Jacob Riis, who through his work attempted to expose conditions in the New York tenements of the late 19th century. By exposing these conditions to those who would otherwise remain unaware – largely middle- and upper-class New Yorkers – Riis hoped to do 'muckraking' journalism that affected positive reform. This idea of muckraking would later be taken up by the sociologist, Gary T. Marx (1972: np) who suggested that sociology as a discipline ought to be on the side of the downtrodden and oppressed by doing sociological research that:

at its best documents conditions that clash with basic values, fixes responsibility for them and is capable of generating moral outrage.

The research conducted by Du Bois and which underpinned *The Philadelphia Negro* (1899) clearly resonates with what Marx (1972) outlines here and with what Riis, a White Danish-American, was successful in accomplishing through journalism coupled with photography. As a study, *The Philadelphia Negro* (1899) though complex and nuanced nevertheless clearly shows that the poverty of Black Philadelphians was not a natural or self-perpetuated condition and was in fact the result of a range of intersectional factors and a symptom of powerful structural forces. Du Bois also showed the devastating impact of continual disadvantage and oppression on Black Philadelphians and the impact of this on Philadelphian society as a whole. In doing so, Du Bois had undoubtedly hoped to document conditions, fix responsibility and generate a response. It is to the detriment of American society in general that his ideas were largely left unattended in his own time and to the detriment of sociology as a discipline that *The Philadelphia Negro* (1899) did not become a classic of the sociological cannon as an exemplar in the doing of sociology. In later work, and particularly in *Black Reconstruction* (1935), Du Bois would outline the complex relationship between race, racial oppression and capitalism. Moreover, his work is notable for foreshadowing what are now routinely accepted sociological lenses including intersectionality, social constructionism, symbolic interactionism and **standpoint theory**. The restoration of Du Bois to the sociological cannon is an important, and, arguably, as yet unfinished project. However, the use and practical application of his ideas is an equally important undertaking and social work, as both an academic and practical discipline, is arguably well placed to meet this task. However, with respect to social work, and with some notable exceptions (see Hollinsworth, 2020), Du Bois has also been left largely unattended. Nevertheless, he has written much that can be of value when thinking about social work. In this respect, the Du Boisian concepts that will be explored in this chapter are as follows:

> **Standpoint theory** suggests that the perspectives of individuals are rooted in their social and political experiences. A culmination of experiences gives rise to an individual's point of view – or standpoint – through which that person ultimately interprets and understands the world. Standpoint theory is perhaps most associated with diverse iterations of feminist theory.

- The veil
- Double consciousness
- The colour line

There have been many interpretations of the concept of the veil as given by Du Bois. This is true also of Du Bois's conceptualisations of double consciousness and the colour line. It is also true that Du Bois's work has been widely interpreted as having shifted and changed over the course of his career; for example, Du Bois drew on the work and ideas of Marx much more prevalently in his own later work in showing that racial oppression, inequality and disadvantage were symptoms of a global capitalist system and of colonialism. In order to keep things relatively simple and applicable in the context of social work, I intend to 'stack' the concepts noted earlier and I start here with the idea of the veil and locate this in the domain of the psychological. Double consciousness is also treated in this way but with an additional emphasis on the material repercussions of what it means to grapple with a divided and unreconciled self. The colour line and the effects of the colour line are treated economically and sociologically and so, though these ideas may not have been presented quite as neatly or as linearly in Du Bois's own work, it makes sense to present them in this fashion here. As with all the chapters in this book, these complex concepts are presented in simple terms and later related to social work. Materials to encourage the reader to go further and deepen their understanding are offered at the end of the chapter.

The veil

> A **heuristic device** functions as a 'shortcut' and can help us to think through complex problems by offering us a language to ground our understanding in. Stories, metaphors and so on can be termed heuristic in this sense.

In many ways the veil as given by Du Bois can be thought of or used as a **heuristic device** or as a way of thinking about the experiences of people on either side of a racial divide between people of colour and White people. Put more accurately, in *The Souls of Black Folk* (1903), with the veil, Du Bois may be said to have articulated what many or perhaps all people of colour already knew to be true: that their sense of self is much more caught up in, measured by and defined through White people than the other way around, where there may exist ignorance and apathy. The veil then exists for both White people and for people of colour though it functions very differently for each group. For White people, the dominant force in the America of which Du Bois wrote, it causes them to both consciously and unconsciously structure social relations along racial lines; the veil in fact both tacitly and overtly constructs race itself to the detriment of racialised persons. For people of colour, the veil causes them to see and interpret themselves through the inherent negative prism of Blackness that the racism of the veil creates. Du Bois (1903/2007: 7) captures this by asking 'How does it feel to be a problem?', a profound question that cuts to the core of what it feels like to be a person of colour in a predominantly White and often hostile world. This question for Du Bois is also tied up in what was then the United States' very recent history: with Black emancipation came attempts at reconstruction, legitimised segregation via **Jim Crow** and the ongoing framing of the position of Black persons as 'the negro problem'. For Du Bois, the veil is not something that Black people are born with an inherent awareness of, rather awareness develops usually through childhood and usually through encounters with people outside of their immediate families or communities. In *The Souls of Black Folk* (1903/2007), which is threaded through with biography, Du Bois describes his becoming aware of the veil as a child, something which awoke in him

> The **Jim Crow** Laws were state and local laws introduced in the Southern United States in the late 19th and early 20th centuries that enforced racial segregation.

the sense of being seen in a particular way and which also had the effect of his not being seen as a full person. Du Bois (1903/2007: 7) also describes the psychological effects of the veil on Black persons in general, who, aware that they occupy a lesser position in a White American world, aware that they are in effect 'strangers in their own house', must reconcile themselves to a world in which:

> The shades of the prison–house closed round about us all: walls strait and stubborn to the whitest, but relentlessly narrow, tall and unscalable to the sons of night who must plod darkly on in resignation, or beat unavailing palms against the stone, or steadily, half hopelessly, watch the streak of blue above.

Beautifully acquitted, Du Bois conjures the spectre of incarceration and limited options here and describes the devasting personal effects of the veil on people of colour. Moreover, though I have located the idea of the veil in the psychological, there are clear shades of sociological analysis here as Du Bois outlines the real material effects of the veil, which both psychologically but also socially imprisons. There are resonances with Marx's conceptualisation of alienation here also, which we covered in the last chapter as a social condition with clear sociological effects. Moreover, in describing how Black persons learn to define themselves through what the veil signifies, Du Bois pre-empts the symbolic interactionist tradition that we will touch on later, in our chapter on Axel Honneth.

In summarising the veil then, in the first instance, for Du Bois, it is represented by the literal dark skin of Black persons, which acts as a form of physical and tangible separation from their White counterparts. Secondly, and indicative of the society at which Du Bois took aim in his theorising, the veil represents an inability on the part of White Americans to see people of colour as fellow Americans, in effect 'invisibilising' them and their inherent humanity. Thirdly and finally, the veil manifests in the inability of Black persons to see themselves outside of how they are viewed and described by White Americans while also potentially meaning that Black persons see all of White America through the veil as hostile and uncaring at worse, apathetic at best. In further building his analysis, Du Bois extends the effect of the veil and moves towards the idea of double consciousness.

Double consciousness

Having suggested the veil as something that represents a division that creates, reaffirms and lies along racialised lines, experienced by both Black people and White people but experienced very differently with deep psychological impacts for the former and a tendency to shape the exclusionary behaviour of the latter, Du Bois introduced the idea of double consciousness. Double consciousness can be thought of as an effect or consequence of the veil; however, unlike the veil, double consciousness is experienced by people of colour as a deeply riven internal and psychological division and is not experienced by White people, who have no conception of this spilt identity. For Du Bois, the Black American is born with a veil and because of this is 'gifted with second sight' (1903/2007: 8) in the form of a double consciousness. Du Bois (1903/2007: 8–9) describes double consciousness at length in the following terms:

> It is a peculiar sensation, this double-consciousness, this sense of always looking at one's self through the eyes of others, of measuring one's soul by the tape of a world that looks on in amused contempt and pity. One ever feels his two-ness, an American, a Negro; two souls, two thoughts, two unreconciled strivings; two warring ideals in one dark body, whose dogged strength alone keeps it from being torn asunder. The history of the American Negro is the history of this strife – this longing to attain self-conscious manhood, to merge his double self into a better and truer self. In this merging he wishes neither of the older selves to be lost. He does not wish to Africanize America, for America has too much to teach the world and Africa. He wouldn't bleach his Negro blood in a flood of white Americanism, for he knows that Negro blood has a message for the world. He simply wishes to make it possible for a man to be both a Negro and an American without being cursed and spit upon by his fellows, without having the doors of opportunity closed roughly in his face.

This extraordinary passage is probably the most famous written by Du Bois and for good reason. Not only does it accurately capture and reflect the America into which Du Bois was writing, it arguably still resonates there and in many other parts of the world today. Here Du Bois questions what it means to be both Black and American and describes how these facets of identity are separate and often at odds for the Black person in American society. He notes that to be both Black and American manifests as a form of 'two-ness' wherein 'two souls' are in tension in one body. In contrast, for White Americans, no such tension exists, and Whiteness and Americanness are naturally and unquestionably reconciled. This does not mean that White Americans don't or can't suffer or face discrimination or disadvantage on other fronts. However, it does mean that whatever challenges White Americans can face, they face them secure in the knowledge of their identities as Americans. Persons of colour on the other hand wish to be both Black and American, two identities they ostensibly hold yet continually struggle to reconcile. Moreover, for Du Bois, this struggle for the reconciliation of two identities is not merely an internal struggle played out in the consciousness of the Black person, it is reflected back to the Black person via the exclusionary tendencies that stem from what it means to be on the Black side of the veil. In an overarching way, shades of such theorising by Du Bois represent by now well-trodden territory by sociologists and social theorists and speak to how people can find themselves grappling with more than one and perhaps contradictory identities in multiple contexts. Much of double consciousness also foreshadows by now well-established sociological theory including Erving Goffman's ideas about how people present themselves in multiple contexts, a subject we will cover in the chapter on Axel Honneth, along with the effects of Pierre Bourdieu's lesser-known concept of *habitus clivé* or the divided self. Crucially, double consciousness can be extended beyond the context into which Du Bois was writing to consider any society in which racialised or minoritised persons form part of a population.

A complex conceptual offering, alongside being replete with elements of internal struggle it can also be suggested, in part at least, that double consciousness as given by Du Bois has the character of being both a curse *and* a blessing. A curse, in that for Du Bois, in order for Black persons to become fully American within themselves and within America, these two distinct aspects of identity must be both socially and psychologically reconciled so that there is no internal or external contradiction between being Black and being American. Yet, this double consciousness might also be seen as blessing or 'gift' of sorts, the gift of 'second-sight', a gift which uniquely positions people of colour to see the exclusionary nature of a stratified society and therefore know instinctually what to do about it. Moreover, Du Bois notes that the dual identities that underpin the double consciousness of Black Americans must be reconciled without sacrificing one or the other. Persons of colour, Du Bois suggests, do not wish for America to become accommodating at the expense of diversity. Neither do people of colour wish to lose their own distinct identities which, while not homogenous, and rich and diverse in their own right, have much to collectively offer America. For Du Bois then, reconciliation of double consciousness is not about assimilation, rather it is about being able to be both Black and American and for there to be no contradiction or tension between these. The way in which societies prevent this from becoming possible for Black persons manifests in what Du Bois refers to as the colour line.

The colour line

The colour line as a concept does not begin with Du Bois though he did arguably popularise it and it was a concept he returned to both explicitly and implicitly throughout his career. In his essay, 'The Color Line', published in

> **Frederick Douglass** (c. February 1817 or February 1818 to 20 February 1895) was an American social reformer, abolitionist, orator, writer and statesman and one of the most notable leaders of the movement for African-American civil rights in the 19th century.

1881 in *The North American Review*, the American abolitionist and orator, **Frederick Douglass**, wrote about the colour line as manifested in the ongoing discrimination against and mistreatment of Black people in a post-emancipation America (1881: 568):

> In nearly every department of American life they [Black people] are confronted by this insidious influence. It fills the air. It meets them at the work shop and factory, when they apply for work. It meets them at the church, at the hotel, at the ballot-box, and worst of all, it meets them in the jury-box.

Douglass also sketched out how the colour line manifested far beyond interpersonal interactions and mistreatment to ultimately limit the lives of persons of colour in myriad ways, meaning that emancipation from slavery had resulted in limited freedom at best (1881: 568):

> The workshop denies him work, and the inn denies him shelter; the ballot-box a fair vote, and the jury-box a fair trial. He has ceased to be the slave of an individual but in sense has become the slave of society. He may not now be bought and sold like a beast in the market, but he is the trammeled victim of a prejudice, well calculated to repress his manly ambition, paralyze his energies, and make him a dejected and spiritless man, if not a sullen enemy to society, fit to prey upon life and property and to make trouble generally.

This extraordinary and scathing essay by Douglass effectively sets out how the colour line in America operated and what the consequences of the colour line were for Black people who were denied the right to full, free and fair participation in many facets of American society as a result of it. In illuminating prose and essay style, Douglass foreshadows many of Du Bois's own empirical sociological observations and insights in the context of the colour line. This is important to note as in joining the two, Du Bois would effectively go on to empirically demonstrate what Douglass had claimed was happening in America in his essay, several years earlier.

Mentioned several times by Du Bois in *The Philadelphia Negro* (1899), this study effectively showed the broader sociological consequences of the colour line for both people of colour and for Philadelphian society as a whole. For example, in the chapter on 'Color Prejudice', Du Bois (1899: 351) makes explicit the link between continual discrimination and disadvantage and criminal behaviour:

a great amount of crime can be without doubt traced to the discrimination against Negro boys and girls in the matter of employment. Or to put it differently, Negro prejudice costs the city something. The connection of crime and prejudice is, on the other hand, neither simple nor direct. The boy who is refused promotion in his job as porter does not go out and snatch somebody's pocketbook ... The connections are much more subtle and dangerous; it is the atmosphere of rebellion and discontent that unrewarded merit and reasonable but unsatisfied ambition make.

This insight into effective disenfranchisement leading to criminal conduct as a means to achieve what society has denied to persons foreshadows the sociology of criminal behaviour later developed by the sociologist Robert Merton who would go on to theorise something remarkably similar while drawing on the work of Durkheim. Moreover, it both describes how the colour line operates while pointing to at least one of the potential outcomes of the disenfranchisement created by it. This passage by Du Bois shows what the colour line meant for people of colour living in the city of Philadelphia at that time and in the context of employment opportunities. However, Du Bois's analysis goes beyond documenting the very real plight of Black persons in the city to show how the colour line 'costs the city something'. In doing so, he suggests that the disadvantage of the Black people of Philadelphia is ultimately to the disadvantage and detriment of all who occupy the city. Disadvantage comes by way of a vast pool of untapped talent and potential left go to waste at the expense of the city, detriment by way of the 'atmosphere of rebellion and discontent' such social conditions are apt to create. Yet this insight is only one way in which Du Bois documents the sociological effects of the colour line in an early and specific study in the form of *The Philadelphia Negro* (1899). In later work, Du Bois would presciently point to the colour line as a major international problem:

> Robert Merton (4 July 1910 to 23 February 2003) was an American sociologist and is generally considered a founding father of modern sociology and a major contributor to the subfield of criminology.

> The problem of the twentieth century is the problem of the color-line – the relation of the darker to the lighter races of men in Asia and Africa, in America and the islands of the sea.

In this passage from the second essay in *The Souls of Black Folk* (1903/2007: 15), Du Bois makes clear that the colour line affects all persons of colour and on an international level, something he would later flesh out considerably in the context of colonial histories and extractive nature of colonialism. In *Black Reconstruction* (1935) Du Bois would extend his international analysis to consider the plight of international labour and its relationship to the colonial working classes, the latter of whom he suggested would need to secure political and social emancipation as part of a broader project of emancipation before extending this to global labour in general. In this way, Du Bois might be suggested to have been arguing for a dismantlement of the global colour line as part of a broader movement towards the emancipation of the working classes.

'Stacking' concepts as I have in this chapter, I have built towards the colour line by locating both the veil and double consciousness primarily, though not exclusively, in the domain of the psychological. However, what is key to understanding the effects of the colour line as given by Du Bois is understanding that it is not merely a psychological construct, though it may in fact have psychological repercussions. Rather, the colour line results in tangible, material effects for persons of colour or other racialised and/or minority groups. The colour line gives rise to concerning exclusionary effects and affects things like job prospects and employment opportunities, fair treatment in legal proceedings, access to social goods like education and, important from a social work perspective, fair and equitable treatment within services. Finally, while Du Bois was undoubtedly frustrated by the continuing presence of the colour line as a factor in the division of resources and opportunities, he did not appear to think of it as a permanent or immutable structure and so left room for the possibility that it could be exposed, challenged and perhaps ultimately confined to history.

Du Bois and social work

Having sketched some of Du Bois's concepts, it must first be noted that what has been offered here has really only scratched the surface of what Du Bois covered in his lifetime. Nevertheless, there is much in what has been offered that can be related to and used when thinking about social work. If we take first Du Bois's concept of the veil, this can be used to think about social work from a number of relevant perspectives. In the first instance, and regardless of context, it is natural to consider what it might mean to be a racialised or minoritised person who has social work involvement in their life. This can lead us to use Du Bois to reflect and ask questions like: will a social worker view and treat a Black person differently to a White person because of preconceptions or stereotypes? Moreover, will a Black service user come to an interaction with a social worker with a specific view of themselves as a person of colour or of the social worker as a representative of politically recognised profession? These questions are useful for the purposes of reflection and reflective practice and can be used to help social work practitioners and those undertaking training to make use of the Du Boisian concept of the veil as a means of critical interrogation. Moreover, such questions are of critical importance because empirical research consistently shows that racialised and minoritised persons are vastly over-represented among social work service users, which might be said to represent or demonstrate the effects of the veil and an example of the colour line at work. For example, in a study drawn from the Irish context, Coulter (2015: 13) found that:

African families are about seven times more likely to face child protection proceedings than are Irish people, and this figure is likely to be greater if the "Mixed" category includes one African parent, as we have observed it often does.

These are themes which Marovatsanga and Garrett (2024) cover extensively in the context of social work with the Black African diaspora. While beyond the scope of this chapter, it is nevertheless important to question why this is and the sociology of Du Bois can provide a conceptual framework to aid with this questioning.

However, while what has been offered so far may be useful, it must be remembered that social work is not a homogenous profession, and not all social work students are White and so it is also apt to use Du Bois's work to ask how the veil, double consciousness and the colour line might affect a social worker who also happens to be a person of colour, or a social work student studying towards professional qualification who belongs to a minoritised or racialised group. Again, a similar series of reflective prompts can be offered here as a starting point so that we might ask: what challenges might Black or minoritised social work students or practitioners face in day-to-day study or practice? How are such experiences mediated by the veil? Could these challenges lead to a form of double consciousness? These questions are also crucial in a way that goes beyond reflection. In a study by Bernard and colleagues (2011: 72), which looked at diversity and progression among social work students in England, Black and minority ethnic students noted that they experienced:

> a range of discriminatory processes including: being subject to derogatory stereotypes and hostility from practice assessors and other staff members; feeling excluded and isolated; being expected to work harder and to be more capable that their white counterparts . . . One particular theme that a number of students spoke about was their belief that certain accents – particularly African accents – were devalued, and this contributed to negative judgments being made about them by practice assessors and others.

In this example, which draws on student experiences while on practice placement, we can easily identify aspects of Du Boisian sociology. The veil is rendered visible through the way in which these Black and minority ethnic students describe being treated and it is clear they perceive being treated very differently to their White counterparts. The veil as given by Du Bois, the prism through which White people view Black or otherwise minoritised persons also represents the clear potential for inaccuracy and stereotype, something which the student respondents speak about encountering in the given excerpt. There are also elements of double consciousness in what is described as students identifying their accents as a precursor to feeling or being devalued, which in turn requires us to reflect on what it might mean to be both a Black African person and a student social worker and whether or not there is a struggle to reconcile these.

Before finishing with Du Bois and turning next to the colour line specifically, it is worth remembering that the colour line can be viewed as the tangible manifestation of the veil. The colour line has structuring tendencies and is important in the context of the distribution of resources. While it obviously shouldn't be the case, the concept of the colour line suggests that what you can expect to have, get, experience and have access to is mediated by which side of the colour line you are on so that Black or otherwise racialised minoritised persons can expect to find their lives and their ability to take a full and unencumbered part in society stymied. Therefore, taking the colour line as given by Du Bois as a conceptual and analytical tool, it can be used to interrogate contexts wherever instances of oppression or disenfranchisement based on aspects of identity occur. If we briefly revisit *The Philadelphia Negro* (1899), we will remember that Du Bois drew a complex line been the continual disenfranchisement of Black Philadelphians and the same group's criminal behaviour, noting that it 'cost the city something'. If we update this analysis and look just at headline statistics in the UK (GOV.UK, 2023), we can see that:

> [B]lack people were 2.4 times as likely to be arrested as white people – there were 21.2 arrests for every 1,000 black people, and 9.0 arrests for every 1,000 white people.

Yet, without going so far as to claim a correlation, other statistics from the same jurisdictions nevertheless tell us that access to basic resources and social goods is a continuous challenge for Black and minority ethnic persons. For example, Black and minority ethnic workers are more than twice (2.2 times) as likely as White workers to face unemployment (TUC [Trade Union Congress], 2023). Moreover, Black and minority ethnic men face an unemployment rate of 6.3 per cent compared to 3.7 per cent for White men and the youth unemployment rate for young Black and minority ethnic workers stands at 19.2 per cent, compared to 8.8 per cent for young White workers (TUC, 2023). We can also consider that, across the UK, more people from Black, Asian and other minority ethnic backgrounds are likely to be in poverty than White British people (Marmot et al, 2020). Again, space here does not allow for a deeper analysis but even on the surface, when taken together, these statistics give a broad indication of the colour line in action in a developed economy at the expense of racialised and minoritised persons. It also suggests that this costs society something, in this case in the UK. This in turn demonstrates the prescience and continuing relevance of Du Bois as a critical social theorist who, couched in his own lived experience, developed a scholarship of race and racial relations that still rings true. Moreover, in social work theory in general, there has long been a tradition of anti-oppressive and anti-discriminatory practice models, much of which undoubtedly filters down to practice in myriad ways. An exemplar of this can be found in Tedam's (2021) *Anti-Oppressive Social Work Practice*, which, without directly referencing Du Bois, resonates with aspects of his work in various ways. Given that this strong tradition already exists, the admission of Du Boisian sociological theory to the canon of social work theory and in particular to anti-oppressive and anti-discriminatory approaches is arguably long overdue.

Summary

In this chapter we explored the work of W.E.B. Du Bois. At the outset, we noted that Du Bois has not always been given enough attention as a social theorist despite the importance of his contribution and that this was reflective of his lived experiences generally as a Black man in the deeply racially segregated United States of his time. In approaching Du Bois's work, the chapter proceeded by 'stacking' some of his better-known concepts for ease of understanding. In this respect, we saw that the veil for Du Bois is something that people of colour often become aware of as children as a line of difference between themselves and others. In Du Bois's example, the veil existed for both Black and White persons, with White people tending to view Black people in inherently negative ways through the prism of the veil and with Black people seeing a skewed version of themselves in this negative reflection. From here we moved on to consider Du Bois's conceptualisation of double consciousness. We saw that for Du Bois, to be both Black and American represented two distinct strands of identity, often in conflict with each other and in need of reconciliation so that Black Americans could fully assume their identities as Americans. We also saw how this conceptual gift from Du Bois can be extended to help us think about what it might mean to grapple with dual aspects of identity for racialised and minorities persons in multiple contexts, including in multiple scenarios involving social work. Finally, we looked at Du Bois's iteration of the colour line. We saw that the colour line has deep structuring tendencies which in turn have repercussions for resources in terms of what people can reasonably expect to access and avail of as members of a given society. We saw how Du Bois demonstrated the colour line at work through his own empirical, sociological work and how it can be used as an analytical tool to interrogate the conditions of racialised and minoritised persons today.

For students: Exercise box 4

In this chapter we explored the work of W.E.B. Du Bois. To further explore your understanding, consider the following:

1. Think about Du Bois's concept of the veil. What might it mean to feel as though you are viewed and treated differently because of an aspect of your identity?
2. Think about Du Bois's concept of double consciousness. How might this affect people from Black and minority ethnic backgrounds? How can this be considered as part of the social work process?

3. Finally, think about the exclusionary effects of the colour line. How can social workers be mindful of the exclusionary and discriminatory effects of the colour line?

Further reading

- If you would like to read something written by Du Bois himself, *The Souls of Black Folk* is short, accessible and contains many of his key ideas and most famous passages. It is also beautifully written.
- Du Bois, W.E.B. (1903/2007) *The Souls of Black Folk*, Oxford: Oxford University Press.
- This short chapter by David Hollinsworth is very good and will further help flesh out your understanding of Du Bois's contribution.
- Hollinsworth, D. (2020) 'Lifting the veil of our own consciousness: W.E.B. Du Bois and transformative pedagogies for social work', in C. Morley, P. Ablett, P. Noble and S. Cowden (eds) *The Routledge Handbook of Critical Pedagogies for Social Work*, London: Routledge, pp 45–57.

Why not watch!

There are many useful clips on YouTube that may help to flesh out and deepen your understanding. One which is particularly useful is called 'An introduction to W.E.B. Du Bois' The Souls of Black Folk – Macat Sociology Analysis' and is published by the Macat educational YouTube channel. It is available here: https://youtu.be/tvE3Ft10h2w?si=V7RD2kAp03tzYaRL

Why not listen!

Podcasts are a great way to learn! The following podcast episode is part of the 'Philosophy Talk' series and called 'W.E.B. Du Bois'. It is available here: https://www.philosophytalk.org/shows/web-du-bois

Chapter references

Anderson, E. and Massey, D.S. (2001) 'The sociology of race in the United States', in E. Anderson and D.S. Massey (eds) *Problem of the Century: Racial Stratification in the United States*, New York: Russell Sage, pp 3–12.

Bernard, C., Fairtlough, A., Fletcher, J. and Ahmet, A (2011) *Diversity and Progression Among Social Work Students in England*, London: Goldsmiths University.

Coulter, C. (2015) *The Child Care Law Reporting Project: Final Report*, Dublin: The Child Care Law Reporting Project.

Douglass, F. (1881) 'The color line', *The North American Review*, 132(295): 567–77.

Du Bois, W.E.B. (1899) *The Philadelphia Negro: A Social Study*, Philadelphia: University of Philadelphia.

Du Bois, W.E.B. (1903/2007) *The Souls of Black Folk*, Oxford: Oxford University Press.

Du Bois, W.E.B. (1935) *Black Reconstruction: An Essay Toward a History of the Part which Black Folk Played in the Attempt to Reconstruct Democracy in America, 1860–1880*, New York: Harcourt, Brace and Company.

GOV.UK. (2023) *Ethnicity facts and figures: Arrests*. Available from: https://www.ethnicity-facts-figures.service.gov.uk/crime-justice-and-the-law/policing/number-of-arrests/latest/ [Accessed 26 June 2024].

Lewis, D.L. (1993) *W.E.B. Du Bois: Biography of a Race, 1868–1919*, New York: Henry Holt.

Marmot, M., Allen, J., Boyce, T., Goldblatt, P. and Morrison, J. (2020) *Health Equity in England: the Marmot Review 10 years on*, London: Institute of Health Equity.

Marovatsanga, W. and Garrett, P.M. (2024) *Social Work with the Black African Diaspora*, Bristol: Policy Press.

Marx, G.T. (1972) *Research as social criticism from muckraking sociology*. Available from: https://web.mit.edu/gtmarx/www/ascmuck.html [Accessed 26 June 2024].

Tedam, P. (2021) *Anti-Oppressive Social Work Practice*. London: Sage

TUC [Trade Union Congress] (2023) *Jobs and recovery monitor—BME Workers 2023*. Available from: https://www.tuc.org.uk/research-analysis/reports/jobs-and-recovery-monitor-bme-workers-2023 [Accessed 26 June 2024].

For instructors: A set of slides that accompany this chapter can be accessed through the book webpage: https://policy.bristoluniversitypress.co.uk/critical-theory-for-social-work.

5

Jürgen Habermas and social work

Biographical note

Jürgen Habermas was born in Gummersbach, Rhine Province, Germany on 18 June 1929. He was born with a cleft palate that required surgeries during childhood. Habermas has made the case that his speech impediment caused him to look inward and to think very deeply about the importance of communication, a theme that would characterise much of his work. It is frequently mentioned in biographical notes about Habermas that as a young person he was part of the Hitler Youth. However, it must be remembered that this was extremely common among German youths of Habermas's generation and Habermas, like so many others, was horrified by the inhumane cruelty of the war. In the post-war period, Habermas turned to intellectual inquiry and had a wide range of interests. In 1949, he studied philosophy, psychology and German literature in Gottingen, Zurich and then in Bonn where he honed his use of critique. He earned his doctorate in Bonn in 1954. In 1956 he became associated with the famous Frankfurt School or Institute for Social Research where he studied philosophy and sociology under the critical theorists Max Horkheimer and Theodor W. Adorno. However, he became disillusioned with what he saw as the pessimism of the Frankfurt School and left to develop his own ideas. He later returned to take over from Max Horkheimer as Chair of Philosophy and Sociology. After a period as Director of the Max Planck Institute for the Study of the Scientific-Technical World in Starnberg, beginning in 1971 and ending in 1983, he retuned yet again to his chair at the Frankfurt School where he remained until retirement. Habermas remains active and publishing at the time of writing with a book entitled *A New Structural Transformation of the Public Sphere and Deliberative Politics* published in 2023. Though Habermas has written prolifically, key texts by Habermas in the context of this chapter include *The Theory of Communicative Action: Volume One: Reason and the Rationalization of Society* (1984a) and *The Theory of Communicative Action: Volume Two: Lifeworld and Systems, a Critique of Functionalist Reason* (1984b).

Introduction

With Habermas, we jump forward to a theorist who helped theorise modernity by both looking back at what had gone before and by looking at what surrounded him. It would be difficult to overestimate the impact on social theory that Jürgen Habermas has had at the end of the 20th and beginning of the 21st centuries and he can rightly be referred to as an 'OG' of critical theory and in particular of the critical theory associated with the Frankfurt School, though he would take this in new directions and break with it in some respects. As a theorist, Habermas's

53

allegiance can be difficult to pin down, as noted by Bryson (2019: 65) who tells us that:

> With Marx, Weber, and Marcuse, Habermas shares a critique of technical or instrumental rationality, positivism, bureaucracy, capitalism, ideology, and domination. With Foucault, Lacan, and Derrida, Habermas recognizes the importance of language and meaning-making. What distinguishes Habermas from classical and contemporary social theorists alike is that he retains a belief in political consensus forged on the basis of collectively negotiated and legitimated values.

As can be seen, Habermas clearly shares some common ground with theorists associated with both modernist and postmodernist perspectives. Yet, characteristic of his break with the pessimism of the Frankfurt School and of his criticisms of postmodernist theory, Habermas shuns the overt pessimism of the former and the reductive nature of the latter and keeps faith with Enlightenment principles by believing in the prospect of consensus through communication. Indeed, in critiquing some aspects of postmodern thought, Habermas and Ben-Habib (1981: 11) note that:

> I think that instead of giving up modernity and its project as a lost cause, we should learn from the mistakes of those extravagant programs which have tried to negate modernity.

Postmodernists, for Habermas, ignore everyday life and its practices, things which Habermas finds absolutely central (Ritzer and Stepnisky, 2013). Chief among these for Habermas is communication and how we communicate with one another. With this in mind the core Habermasian concepts to be covered in this chapter are all related to communication in some fundamental way and are as follows.

We will start by sketching Habermas's theory of society by covering:

• The lifeworld and the system.

From here we will focus on communication by focusing on:

• Communicative action and ideal speech; and
• Strategic action.

In general, when reading about Habermas in the context of social work, it has been my experience that authors tend to start with Habermas's ideas on communication before proceeding to discuss and explore his concepts of lifeworld and system. However, I approach this chapter in reverse order with a view to first describing the issues that have arisen in the lifeworld and system as Habermas sees them before then exploring his theories of communication and how this might ameliorate these. As with all the chapters in this book, these complex concepts are presented in simple terms and so materials to encourage the reader to go further and deepen their understanding are offered at the end of the chapter.

The lifeworld and the system

The concepts of lifeworld and system are key to understanding the importance of language and communication in Habermas's work in ways which have huge relevance for social work. This is because the modes of communication in the lifeworld and system are very different and serve very different purposes. In what follows, lifeworld and system are defined separately before being related to one another in the context of Habermas's theory of colonisation of the lifeworld by the system.

Lifeworld

Simply put, lifeworld for Habermas might be taken to mean the things that happen in daily life contexts, outside of formal organisations and in a space characterised by the daily communication that occurs between persons. Houston (2009: 16) describes the lifeworld of Habermas in the following terms:

> Lifeworld – refers to the subterranean or background reservoir of shared, and often taken for granted, meanings that, through language, shape our personalities and group identities. It is here that we find daily incidents of communicative action.

Key here is the term 'communicative action' which we will come to further on. For now, we can note that this can be taken to mean open, sincere and non-strategic ways of communicating. For Habermas, when we are 'in' the lifeworld our social actions are not dominated by competition and strategy, rather they are characterised by culture, society and personality. By culture, Habermas (1984b: 209) refers to:

> the stock of knowledge upon which participants in communication draw in order to provide themselves with interpretations that will allow them to reach understanding [with one another].

By society, Habermas (1984b: 209) refers to:

> the legitimate orders through which participants in communication regulate their membership in social groups, and thereby secure solidarity.

And by personality, Habermas (1984b: 209) refers to:

> the competences that make subjects capable of speech and action, and thus enable them to participate in processes of reaching understanding, and thereby assert their own identity.

> A **salon** is a gathering of people held by a host usually brought together to discuss things like art, poetry or philosophy. Salons flourished in France throughout the 17th and 18th centuries and were host to many well-known thinkers of the time.

The lifeworld then is where we meet with one another outside of the system, where through shared knowledge we can attempt to interpret and understand each other, through societal structures and social groups we can meet with one another and share solidarity and through personality we can demonstrate who we are to each other in an attempt to be understood. On a broader note, the lifeworld concept can be related to Habermas's (1989) conceptualisation of the public sphere in earlier work in which he attributed great historical significance to the **salons** of Paris and coffeehouses of England as centres of conversation and exchange that played a crucial role in the emergence of what Habermas termed the 'public sphere'.

System

The system has a very different texture to the lifeworld and communication is also very different here, being characterised by 'strategic action', which we will come to further on. For now, we can note communication via strategic action is likely to be less open and more adversarial than communication through communicative action. For Habermas, when we are in the system, we are in a space that is preoccupied primarily with material reproduction. Houston (2009: 16) sums this up in the following terms:

> the system ... refers to areas of life that are organized and controlled by the State. Formative here are the political and economic subsystems that govern important aspects of our lives. Whereas the lifeworld is concerned with cultural integration and socialization, the system focuses on material reproduction. Consequently, it is dominated by power, money and strategic action.

> **Instrumental rationality** denotes a way of thinking that focuses on the pursuit of objectives in the most efficient way possible in the context of making the most economically efficient decisions possible.

Houston's (2009) description of the system makes a good starting point and captures the essential nature of the system as given by Habermas. The system is dominated by power, money and modes of communication that favour strategic action. We might say that the system is composed of formal organisations, such as governments, corporations, political parties, unions and courts. However, it is also possible to detect two closely connected systems at work in modern liberal democracies: the first being state institutions and institutions connected to the state and the second being markets in which **instrumental rationality** and strategic action are key to the realisation of profit.

Though it is possible to think of Habermas's concepts of lifeworld and system as empirical categories rooted in social institutions, they are arguably largely most useful as heuristic devices that can help us think about how society is organised. Habermas, as cited in Baxter (1987: 53) notes this by making the suggestion that we should:

> consider society an entity that in the course of [social] evolution is differentiated as system as well as lifeworld. System evolution can be evaluated according to the heightening of a system's capacity for steering or control, while the separation of culture, society, and personality indicates the level of development of a symbolically structured lifeworld.

Habermas suggests that though the system initially emerged from the lifeworld, as capitalist societies have developed, the lifeworld and the system became more and more distinct from one another, eventually separating entirely or 'decoupling'. Moreover, as traditions couched in religious practice receded and secularisation increased, the lifeworld, a sphere built on shared customs, practices and understandings, became weakened and therefore vulnerable. Having a functioning system and a separate lifeworld as part of how the world is made up seems reasonable and maybe even necessary. In the lifeworld people share culture, integrate with one another and communicate more or less openly. The system, with its focus on efficiencies and strategic action, provides the necessary social, economic and political architecture to allow for the material reproduction that can allow both spheres to flourish. However, as the lifeworld has weakened and the system has gotten ever stronger, things have become problematic and the rational logic of the system has begun to characterise, shape and colonise the lifeworld.

The colonisation of the lifeworld by the system

Blaug (1995: 426) notes that:

> In the modern social world, communicative reason is forever under attack from instrumentalism. Areas of our daily lives such as childrearing and family health thus become increasingly rule governed and professionalized. Habermas describes this as a process of colonization, whereby our communicative practices are systematically undermined by instrumental ways of thinking.

Taking forward Blaug's (1995) interpretation of Habermas, it is not hard to look at modern, liberal democracies and see that logics dictated by rational or market-based principles have begun to dominate much of social life. This is because a weakened lifeworld is vulnerable to manipulation through instrumental rationality. We can take the example of 'care'. Care is close to the heart of what social workers do in myriad ways. Care as a word evokes a sense of love, support, looking after one another, looking out for another, wanting each other to do and be well. These are all things that arguably belong firmly in the lifeworld. Yet, in the social work context care has begun to be affected by the instrumental rationality of the system. Appropriate care is measured or evaluated for efficiency. Moreover, through the proliferation of things like private fostering services, care has become commodified and imbued with the potential for profit. Beyond social work, care is bought and sold in the context of old age, childhood, psychology and counselling services and in many more contexts. Using Habermas's conception of lifeworld and system, it could be argued that this is indicative of the colonisation of the lifeworld by the system. Houston (2009: 17) sums this process of colonisation up in the following terms:

> Having uncoupled from the lifeworld, the all-powerful system re-enters it ... to colonize its functions. This means that instrumentality, rationality, money, bureaucracy and power – the trappings of the system – usurp communicative action as the chief means for resolving issues and problems in the lifeworld. As a consequence, social life becomes increasingly monetarized, commodified and bureaucratized.

Houston (2009) develops the idea that the colonisation of the lifeworld by the system ultimately represents the colonisation of lifeworld functions. In the lifeworld, we enjoy the freedom of knowing that any issue is open to scrutiny and that problems can be resolved through reasonable and well-intentioned communication. However, if in the lifeworld we were free to meet with one another, talk openly and resolve our differences through dialogue, in the system we resolve our differences using strategic action and instrumental rationality. Thus, we are in effect alienated from many of the acts that Habermas believes make us human.

Thinking about social work

In discussing what the colonisation of the lifeworld by the system looks like in the context of social work, Baianstovu and Ablett (2020: 457–458) note that:

> The incursion can be seen in the shift in social work's knowledge base from critical social science and the humanities to psychology and management.

Taking a lead from Baianstovu and Ablett (2020), when using Habermas's theory of the lifeworld and system to think about social work it can be useful to think about social work's functions. Many of the issues that social workers encounter in their daily work are inherently human and require human responses. Things like addiction, family support and care, child protection issues, issues with mental illness or mental health, disability, loss and bereavement – these are all things that require a human response. Moreover, these are all aspects of life that belong, or certainly that belonged, to the lifeworld. However, they are also aspects of life that have become increasingly bureaucratised and the response of social work to these issues has arguably become bureaucratised through the instrumental rationality associated with managerialist approaches to social work practice. Habermas himself pointed to this as evidence of the colonisation of the lifeworld by the system, noting how responses based on instrumental rationality to those experiencing real human need erode and dissolve care based on compassion, empathy and understanding. However, Habermas also sees the potential for restoring balance between the lifeworld and the system. Key to this for Habermas is how we communicate.

Communicative and strategic action

Having read this far, you will already have an understanding of the terms communicative and strategic action. However, in this next section of the chapter we dig a little deeper into these concepts and show how they can be useful when thinking about how we do communication in social work. In first thinking about how and why we communicate, Houston (2009: 14) notes that:

> Habermas ... has taken the 'linguistic turn' ... he sees language as the key medium for constructing reality. From this standpoint, he has made a number of very important observations about the way we communicate with one another. Central, here, are speakers' attempts to validate what they say through reasoned argument.

So, for Habermas, through language we construct and share reality. However, things are not that simple and in order to be understood, we have to enter into communication with each other in a meaningful way. This brings us to Habermas's ideas about validation or validity claims when communicating. For Habermas, when we talk to one another in a reasoned way, we try to make ourselves understood through three validity claims; though we may not do all three of these each time we communicate.

Arguing the case based on evidence

The first way we can attempt to validate ourselves is to argue the case based on evidence. In daily life contexts this is likely to be evidence based on observation and experience so that I might argue that all fish live in water in good faith based on the evidence I have seen that this is the case. I may also enter into more complex conversation where I draw from evidence based on what I have read or watched or studied about. However, outside of daily life contexts, presenting a sincere argument based on evidence has clear and obvious implications for social work practice and the work that social workers do can act as a way to validate the decisions they make as decisions made in good faith.

Validation based on sincerity

A further way that Habermas proposes we can validate what we say when communicating is through being sincere so that what we express is wholly commensurate with what we feel and with our actions in as much as this is possible. It is important to remember that Habermas is not talking about merely giving the impression of sincerity here and that people are likely to be alert to occasions where we are being less than sincere. In daily life contexts we will have all experienced occasions where we felt that some person or persons were not being sincere and where we were therefore not inclined to validate what they were telling us. We have probably been less than sincere with people in our own lives. Yet, sincerity can be taken beyond daily life contexts too and can potentially be a powerful tool in social work. If the people that social workers work with feel that they are being communicated with sincerely, this can be a powerful building block for constructing relationships and trust and this is likely to hold true even where there is disagreement over a course of action.

Morally appropriate statements

This validity claim adds an important qualifier to the previous two. Evidence and sincerity are ultimately rendered moot where the moral appropriateness of a statement or statements is clearly lacking. In other words, there are some things that may be so abhorrent that they are not up for reasonable discussion. However, Habermas takes the idea of moral appropriateness in a different direction, and it functions as a form of validity in its own right. Effectively, it means that to validate what I am saying, I can appeal to the ethical dimension of my argument so that if someone were to argue that poverty was inevitable and so should be accepted, I might argue that there was no moral or ethical reason for poverty to exist. The moral appropriateness of statements also has clear implications for social work as a profession with a well-defined ethical base. Social workers are in effect guided by a code of ethics and so can draw on this in their decision making and in their communication with service users and other professionals in order to validate what they are saying. In his own words, Habermas (1984b: 188) characterises this process in the following terms:

> Truth claims. The utterance must be true in the sense that what it refers to exists, i.e. that it can be observed or verified from all the lifeworld perspectives that the participating actors may hold.
> Validity claims. The utterance should actually consider the legitimate normative context to which it must apply.
> Honesty claims. The intent that the speaker manifests must be uttered with a certain degree of sincerity.

Habermas suggests that when we communicate with each other, we want to be heard, understood and ultimately, we want to reach agreement. He further suggests that we can mobilise empathy to help us in this quest. Communicating is this way is clearly a tall order but, for Habermas, this is how we would and should communicate under the right conditions, conditions that are or were found in the lifeworld. If and when we do manage to communicate in this way, using reasoned argument based on evidence, being sincere in what we say and appealing to moral appropriateness, we engage in what Habermas describes as communicative action with the potential to arrive at an ideal speech situation.

Communicative action and ideal speech

Houston (2009:15) notes that:

> Communicative action occurs when two or more individuals reach a consensual understanding on goals and actions. This form of speech acts as a coordinating mechanism facilitating the expression of all three validity claims and reasoned argument.

So, for Habermas, when people are in a position to engage in reasoned debate using the three validity claims described earlier and when people are able to arrive at agreement or understanding as a result of this process, communicative action has occurred. This clearly devolves on the prospect of good communication and the willingness of all parties to invest in the process described. In reality, this may often be a difficult path to chart; however, Habermas is firm in his thesis that people generally possess an inbuilt desire to be understood and to seek agreement and he doesn't merely state this as a position that he is taking apropos of nothing, rather he draws on the sociology of Max Weber, **Émile Durkheim** and **George Herbert Mead** to give weight to his argument. Building on the prospect for communicative action, Habermas describes what he terms as an ideal speech situation wherein consensus is reached on the strength of argument, where persons who are able to do so are allowed to engage in the process, where questioning and problematising is allowed, where people can express their attitudes and beliefs respectfully and where people can make suggestions (Houston, 2009).

> **Émile Durkheim** (15 April 1858 to 15 November 1917) was a French sociologist. Durkheim formally established the academic discipline of sociology and is commonly cited as one of the principal architects of modern social science, along with both Karl Marx and Max Weber.

> **George Herbert Mead** (27 February 1863 to 26 April 1931) was an American philosopher, sociologist and psychologist, primarily affiliated with the University of Chicago.

Strategic action

Whereas the communicative action resulting in an ideal speech situation is perhaps the goal or ambition, there can also be barriers that arise from the way people communicate and so it is important from Habermas's perspective to avoid using what he terms strategic action when communicating. Strategic action comes via the system to the lifeworld and can colonise and affect how we communicate with one another. On strategic action, Houston (2009: 16) notes:

> Strategic action is commonplace in business and professional life. Here, it can be purely functional, in the sense that corporate objectives have to be met and business plans conceived to guide the employee's actions. However, strategic action can also take the form of one-upmanship, courting favour with the boss and creating alliances when rumours abound of takeover bids and so on.

Strategic action may have a place in the overall world of communication but as it is described here by Houston (2009) it would certainly count as bad communication in many contexts and certainly in the context of social work. Strategic action is clearly aligned with the instrumental rationality of the system yet even in that context it appears as less than ideal. To avoid strategic action, it is necessary to avoid task and efficiency-oriented communication where a human response is required. Likewise, avoiding deliberately closed off or deceitful communication, adversarial or combative forms of communication or communication based solely in impression management is necessary to avoid strategic action and enter into more open forms of communication.

Thinking about social work

There are very clear and obvious ways in which Habermas's ideas about communication are relevant when thinking about social work. Communicative action is perhaps what social workers will and should aspire to. Yet, the instrumental rationality of the system has undeniably begun to characterise social work, and this will undoubtedly affect how social workers communicate. Baianstovu and Ablett (2020: 451) sum this up in the following terms:

> Consensus in a service delivery context, requires that every person be afforded the opportunity for his or her personal situation and needs to be voiced and heard. Nevertheless, social workers in public institutions are not given the options of communicating with clients in the varying ways needed to reach mutual understanding across socioeconomic, cultural, religious and normative differences.

Baianstovu and Ablett (2020) suggest here that social workers are not given the option to or freedom of engaging in communicative action with the people they they work with. Furthermore, communicative action is something that takes time. Moreover, Baianstovu and Ablett (2020) suggest the varying ways of reaching mutual understanding may be out of reach. Given that communication is the bedrock of social work practice, this situation as described by Baianstovu and Ablett (2020) requires deep interrogation. Taken together, Habermas's theory of lifeworld and system and his substantial contribution to thinking on communication offer excellent conceptual and analytical tools through which to begin this interrogation. Moreover, even in practice contexts where it is difficult to fully mobilise Habermas's theory of communicative action with respect to arriving at consensus, it should remain possible to draw from evidence when making a case, to remain sincere even where what is being said is not well taken and to be morally and ethically appropriate when making statements while also appealing to moral appropriateness to help guide decisions. In this respect, Habermas's theory of communicative action can make a valuable reflective tool in social work.

Summary

In this chapter we have explored the work and ideas of the philosopher and social theorist Jürgen Habermas and we have related these to social work. We started by exploring Habermas's conceptualisations of the lifeworld and the system; noting that the lifeworld is where people integrate and communicate through culture, society and personality whereas in the context of the system we find the formal organisations of the state and of the market. With respect to social work, we noted that many of the people social workers will encounter will be experiencing things that require a human response. However, we saw how Habermas's suggestion that the lifeworld has become colonised by the system is apparent in social work, which has become highly bureaucratised and prone to the instrumental rationality of the system. From here we explored Habermas's work on communication. We explored how Habermas believed that people generally strive to reach agreement and to be understood and that this was potentially possible through communicative action which could lead to consensus through an ideal speech situation.

For students: Exercise box 5

In this chapter we explored the work of Jürgen Habermas. To further explore your understanding, consider the following:

1. Think about Habermas's conception of the lifeworld and the system. Make a list of the kinds of things you think fit in each. These could be activities, institutions or practices. Where does social work fit?
2. Think about communicative action and strategic action. Can you think of a time in your life when you used either? Can you think of a time when either style of communication was used by someone else with you? What kind of communication do social workers use?

Further reading
- If you would like to read something written by Habermas himself, this recent article makes a good starting point:
- Habermas, J. (2022) 'Reflections and hypotheses on a further structural transformation of the political public sphere', *Theory, Culture & Society*, 39(4): 145–71.
- Referred to throughout the chapter, this chapter in an edited collection by Stan Houston provides an excellent synopsis of Habermas's relevance to social work:
- Houston, S. (2009) 'Jurgen Habermas', in M. Gray and S. Webb (eds) *Social Work Theories and Methods*, London: Sage, pp 13–23.

Why not watch!

There are many useful clips on YouTube that may help to flesh out and deepen your understanding. One that is particularly useful is called 'Habermas: the structural transformation of the public sphere'.

It is published by Then & Now and is available here: https://www.youtube.com/watch?v=R1K46oK3xTU&t=201s

Why not listen!

Podcasts are a great way to learn! The following podcast is part of the 'Philosophise This!' series and covers Habermas and the public sphere. It is available here: https://www.philosophizethis.org/podcast/the-public-sphere

Chapter references
Baianstovu, R. and Ablett, P. (2020) 'The transformation and integration of society: developing social pedagogy through Jürgen Habermas' theory of communicative action', in C. Morley, P. Ablett, P. Noble and S. Cowden (eds) *The Routledge Handbook of Critical Pedagogies for Social Work*, London: Routledge, pp 450–64.

Baxter, H. (1987) 'System and life-world in Habermas's "Theory of Communicative Action"', *Theory and Society*, 16(1): 39–86.

Blaug, R. (1995) 'Distortion of the face to face: communicative reason and social work practice', *British Journal of Social Work*, 25: 423–39.

Bryson, S. (2019) 'Can the lifeworld save us from neoliberal governmentality? Social work, critical theory, and Habermas', *The Journal of Sociology & Social Welfare*, 46(3): 4.

Habermas, J. (1984a) *The Theory of Communicative Action (Part I. GB)*, Cambridge: Polity Press.

Habermas, J. (1984b) *The Theory of Communicative Action (Part II. GB)*, Cambridge: Polity Press.

Habermas, J. (1989) *The Structural Transformation of the Public Sphere An Inquiry into a Category of Bourgeois Society*. Cambridge, MA: MIT Press.

Habermas, J. and Ben-Habib, S. (1981) 'Modernity versus postmodernity', *New German Critique*, 22: 3–14.

Houston, S. (2009) 'Jurgen Habermas', in Gray, M. and Webb, S. (eds) *Social Work Theories and Methods*, London: Sage, pp 13–23.

Ritzer, G. and Stepnisky, J. (2013) *Sociological Theory*, New York: McGraw Hill.

For instructors: A set of slides that accompany this chapter can be accessed through the book webpage: https://policy.bristoluniversitypress.co.uk/critical-theory-for-social-work.

6

Axel Honneth and social work

Biographical note

Axel Honneth was born on 18 July 1949, in Essen, West Germany. He studied in Bonn, Bochum, Berlin and in Munich under Jürgen Habermas and he taught at the Free University of Berlin and the New School before moving to the Goethe University Frankfurt in 1996. His connection with the Frankfurt School and with critical theory stem from the fact that he studied under Habermas and between 2001 and 2018 was director of the Institute for Social Research, originally at the University of Frankfurt. Honneth's work has focused on social, political and moral philosophy and the core of much of his work focuses on the importance of recognition and respect. As a theorist, while Honneth's work does share some concerns with more postmodernist theorists, particularly in the context of identity, it is most closely aligned with traditional modernity as he tried to develop a theory of recognition upon which mutually beneficial social and economic relationships could be based. For the purposes of this chapter, the key text in focus is *The Struggle for Recognition: The Moral Grammar of Social Conflicts* (1995) which develops many ideas that can prove useful when thinking about social work.

Introduction

Honneth is a theorist whose ideas have captured the social work imagination and this is evident through not only the contributions his work has fostered in the social work literature but also through the lively debate that characterises much of this (see Houston and Dolan, 2008; Garrett, 2009; Webb, 2010; Houston and Montgomery, 2017; Niemi, 2021 for just some examples). This is testament to the fact that the ideas Honneth presents have a closeness to and applicability for social work. One of his core ideas is that societies should organise by developing strong relationships based on mutual recognition and that not doing so can lead to non-recognition and misrecognition, which in turn creates conflict. At the outset it is important to state that for Honneth, although his theory of recognition is woven through the fabric of the everyday in the form of interpersonal interaction and the recognition of identities, it is also a theory of society and an appeal to **political economy**. Recognition for Honneth then has implications for how we treat one another in everyday instances while also having implications

> **Political economy** is the study of how politics affects the economy and how the economy in turn shapes politics. At its core it is concerned with how resources are distributed.

Nancy Fraser (born 20 May 1947) is an American philosopher, critical theorist and feminist. She is arguably one of the most important thinkers of the later 20th and early 21st centuries and has engaged with the concept of recognition at length in her work.

Erving Goffman (11 June 1922 to 19 November 1982) was a Canadian-born American sociologist who, due to the interpersonal focus of his work, can be associated with the symbolic interactionist tradition. Goffman's output has been hugely influential and continues to form a core component of sociological inquiry and education today.

for the distribution of wealth and goods in society and so directly impacts upon struggles for recognition as struggles for social justice. Moreover, though Honneth recognises that redistributive justice is essential in the context of social injustices, he refuses to separate interpersonal forms of recognition from redistributional recognition as discrete categories on the basis that in his theory of recognition, the latter can be thought of as a component of the former. This runs counter to other important theorists of recognition such **Nancy Fraser** who felt that it was important to have a separate and distinct category covering economic injustices. Somewhat uniquely, Fraser and Honneth (2003) debated this together in *Redistribution or Recognition?: A Political–Philosophical Exchange*. Nevertheless, for the purposes of gaining a general understanding, whether considered at a macro level or at a micro level, recognition as given by Honneth provides a useful tool for thinking about social work. With this in mind, this chapter will cover Honneth's theory of recognition in detail, covering self-recognition, misrecognition and non-recognition while also considering the factors that can lead to good, progressive and appropriate forms of recognition. This chapter will also briefly introduce the work of two other theorists, George Herbert Mead and **Erving Goffman** and relate these to Honneth's work.

Symbolic interactionism

We start by briefly introducing the tradition of symbolic interactionism through the work of George Herbert Mead. Not only was Mead's work on symbolic interactionism formative for Honneth's own theory of recognition, it is also a useful place from which to start in building up our own understanding. Effectively, symbolic interactionism is a perspective in sociology that sees society as the product of shared symbols. The social world is therefore constructed by the meanings that individuals attach to events and social interactions, and these symbols are transmitted across the generations through language. Consider for a moment the set of symbols represented in Figure 6.1.

Do you know what these symbols mean? If yes, *how* do you know, where did your understanding come from? You can be reasonably sure that you did not

Figure 6.1: Signs and symbols

arrive in the world with an inherent understanding of these symbols and that understanding does not arise in a vacuum. Maybe there is a symbol here that you are not so sure of or that could have more than one meaning. In simple terms, symbolic interactionism and the work of Mead suggests that our understanding of the world and through this our 'self' is formed over time and through taking on the perspectives of others. In doing so, we gain an internalised understanding of social expectations, rules and norms (Houston and Dolan, 2008). A central concept of symbolic interactionism is the 'self', which develops through our interactions with others and allows us to have some sense of what the effects of our actions might be. Moreover, symbolic interactionism in general makes the claim that a person or an 'actor's' ability to act upon and interpret the world, their very sense of self in fact, emerges from the ongoing process of communication with others. For Honneth's theory of recognition, this is an important building block because it demonstrates that our identities are intimately intertwined with everyday acts of recognition. Our 'selfs' are reflected in the reaction of others towards us, we in turn act and react. This can happen in ways that recognise, misrecognise or fail to recognise the other.

Recognition theory

Having established through symbolic interactionism that people in society understand their social worlds through communication and the exchange of meaning through language and symbols, we can next turn our attention to recognition. For Honneth, what might be called 'good' recognition devolves on three core concepts: love (in intimate and private relationships but also in a general sense), respect (of rights) and esteem (through opportunities to participate). Houston and Dolan (2008) drawing on Honneth (1995) present these three forms of recognition in the following terms:

(1) recognition of the subject's right to be treated with positive regard or affectionate care; (2) recognition of the subject's entitlement to a wide-ranging body of legal rights; and (3) recognition of the subject's attributes or strengths by a community of interest.

So, in order for persons to be fully recognised, they must be treated humanely and with care, they must be able to avail of their rights and entitlements and they must be afforded the opportunity to contribute to their society or community. Some of these aspects of recognition are things that may or may not happen in everyday or in micro interactions. For example, a social worker may or may not treat a service user with positive regard. Other aspects of the recognition described above go beyond micro and interpersonal interactions and may involve the struggle by some groups for social inclusion or to have their rights recognised and vindicated. This reflects the fact that Honneth's theory of recognition is one where aspects of self-realisation are at play in everyday contexts and also a potentially structuring force that can drive social change and is concerned with social justice. Further on in the chapter, we will briefly explore the prospect of misrecognition or non-recognition and introduce the work of Erving Goffman to help us think about the consequences of misrecognising or not recognising persons. Firstly, however, having sketched a basic understanding of Honneth's theory of recognition as what could be described as 'good' recognition or recognition as it should be when persons experience all three dimensions, we will look in more detail at recognition through love, respect and esteem and relate these to social work.

Recognition through love and social work

For Honneth (1995) love is the primary form of recognition and being loved, cared for and treated with respect builds confidence and self-esteem. Honneth (1995: 95), notes that love:

> represents the first stage of reciprocal recognition, because in it subjects mutually confirm each other with regard to the concrete nature of their needs and thereby recognise each other as needy creatures.

This immediately and obviously chimes with social work and with theories that are prevalent in social work. Take, for example, attachment theory, a staple of social work education which starts from the position that all human beings need to form a secure attachment to a primary caregiver or caregivers, in order to develop healthily. Howe (2009: 43) notes that 'Children who are confident that their parents will be there at times of need and have them in mind grow up to be more independent and autonomous'. In this scenario, the love of a parent or caregiver for a child acts as a form of recognition through which the child gains confidence and self-esteem. Moreover, love as a type of recognition is something that goes beyond forming childhood attachments and can be affirming and confirming for persons throughout their lives. Conversely, to not have love and to not have recognition through love will have obvious effects on a person's sense of self and self-esteem. However, love as recognition is not confined to purely analytical categories that allow social workers to understand why the person or persons they are working with may be presenting in a certain way or experiencing particular types of struggles. Rather, there is a case to be made that love can and should be a texture of the social worker/service user relationship. For example, work by Szeintuch (2022) has recently argued that social work can and should be practised in way that gives rise to and is imbued with what they describe as 'social love'. Moreover, Szeintuch (2022: 474) notes that:

> Be it kindness, solidarity, or any other act of friendship towards fellow humans, I argue that such social work acts are acts of love.

Recognition through love then has clear implications for thinking about social work and can help inform social work assessments by lending depth of understanding to the lives of the people social workers work with while also potentially forming part of relationship building that includes solidarities based on kindness and love.

Recognition through rights and social work

Houston and Dolan (2008: 461) note that 'This second form of recognition, according to Honneth, pivots on the need for mutual respect between actors'. This need for mutual respect between actors is something that is arguably formally enshrined in rights. For Honneth, rights are linked to self-determination so that persons can have a reasonable expectation of being more or less left alone to exercise their rights and freedoms where these do not interfere with the rights and freedoms of another. It should be noted that Honneth is conceptualising rights reasonably expansively here so that rights are conferred in both positive and negative terms in that people should be 'free to' pursue their ends without interference from others while also being 'free from' unreasonable persecution based on aspects of identity such as race, class, gender and so on. These types of rights reflect the civil and political rights described by Marshall (1950) and noted in Chapter 2. They are reflective of Enlightenment thinking but stop somewhat short of conferring social rights, which is in keeping with Honneth's overall approach.

Social work is often conferred with the moniker of being a 'rights-based profession'. The social work mandate in the context of rights is captured in international definitions and codes of ethics across jurisdictions, and students studying social work are introduced early on to the concept of rights and advocacy work. Clearly then, Honneth's dimension of recognition through rights has clear relevance for social work. Like recognition through love, this relevance arguably has two components. The first of these is where social workers work to secure and affirm social user rights through advocacy approaches. I have noted elsewhere that '"social advocacy" is almost always concerned with helping disempowered cohorts to realise rights, and in this way, it represents an avenue for empowerment' (Whelan, 2020: 44). Equally, Leadbetter (2002: 201) has noted that:

> Empowerment and advocacy are both concerned with a shift of power or emphasis towards meeting the needs and rights of people who otherwise would be marginalized or oppressed.

Suffice to say then that in this dimension, Honneth's theory of recognition through rights has obvious relevance in the work that social workers do. The second area where recognition through rights has relevance for social work comes through social workers themselves as professionals who are in a position to affect or otherwise respect the rights of those they work with. Niemi (2021: 2804) notes this simple proposition in the following terms:

> Evidently, care professionals of all kinds should respect client and patient rights, including the right to self-determination.

Social workers can have a powerful impact on the rights of persons in positive and negative terms. In this respect, starting from a position where the social work professional recognises and respects a services user's rights can constitute a firm building block in the context of relationship building. So, whether working on behalf of a person to help them secure and realise their rights or whether simply respecting the rights of persons in the work that they do, Honneth's theory of recognition through rights provides a useful focal point and reflective tool with which social workers can think through action.

Recognition through esteem and social work

People gain recognition through esteem by having opportunities to participate in or contribute to their society or community through a common goal or purpose commensurate with their abilities. Here, the nature of the goal or purpose is arguably less important than the opportunity for involvement. Participation is broadly rendered here and could mean paid employment, voluntary work or participating in clubs and activities. Crucially, esteem from others fosters and bolsters self-esteem and self-efficacy. Moreover, esteem can be rooted in the concept of reciprocity so that those who get esteem are more likely to give it also, meaning the benefit of receiving esteem is likely to have a multiplier effect. Like recognition through love and respect, recognition through esteem has clear implications for thinking about social work on two levels. When people don't have adequate opportunities to participate meaningfully in their community, this can lead to feelings and experiences of exclusion, detachment, poor self-esteem, of alienation or of being effectively othered. 'Othering' can be overt and purposeful and is defined as a discursive practice where the difference of others is used to affirm one's own identity (Jun, 2019). Characteristics that are 'othered' can vary and might be based on employment status, disability, race or ethnicity, social class or many other factors. Yet things can also be much more subtle, and people can be left out or excluded through the barriers society places on them; for example, a physically disabled person might be excluded from opportunities for recognition through esteem because of something as seemly innocuous as the built environment. In either case the effects of being othered or excluded and thereby not having adequate opportunity to affirm oneself or to reciprocally affirm others can have a telling impact on a person's sense of self. Social workers are likely to meet with people who have been excluded or othered in some way: people living with or experiencing addiction, people who have had negative contact with the criminal justice system, people with disabilities or who are suffering with mental illness or poor mental health. For this reason, thinking about the importance of esteem or the lack thereof in the lives of the people that social workers work with offers explanatory potential and the opportunity to feel and display empathy. A second way in which recognition through esteem can prove an important consideration for social workers is within the service user/social worker relationship itself, although this can be difficult as noted by Niemi (2021: 2804):

> Unfortunately, esteem shows often as a problem in the realm of social work. The abilities of and possibilities for clients to earn esteem may be limited … What is more, there are client groups for which it is especially difficult to get esteem. It is especially difficult for former prisoners, alcoholics and drug addicts to get work and earn esteem. Disabled persons and representatives of marginal groups suffer from problems of a similar kind. The use of social services itself may serve as a negative stigma that causes disesteem.

According to Niemi (2021) here, opportunities to foster esteem may be difficult to come by. Moreover, esteem may be more or less hard to come by for particular groups and being involved with social services may itself be disesteeming. Nevertheless, it should at least be possible for social workers themselves, where warranted and appropriate, to offer esteem to the people they work with in the context of the social worker/service user relationship while fostering opportunities for esteem elsewhere where possible.

Misrecognition and non-recognition

Misrecognition and non-recognition in the context of Honneth's theorising on the importance of recognition may seem self-explanatory but they are worth exploring briefly while teasing out some of the implications. If positive and affirming recognition by others shapes identity positively, misrecognition or non-recognition can shape identity negatively. To be misrecognised is perhaps to have some aspect of your identity misunderstood, ignored or mischaracterised. To have some aspect of your identity not be recognised at all may mean that your rights are being infringed upon. To give some examples of what this might look like in practice, consider that in Ireland, same-sex sexual activity was only decriminalised in 1993. This meant that any sexual identity outside of heterosexual relationships was effectively not recognised as valid or legal. This speaks to a form of non-recognition in that law did not recognise same-sex relationships as valid but also of misrecognition due to the fact that same-sex sexual activity was criminalised for being seeing as deviant or amoral. However, bearing out Honneth's thesis of how campaigns for recognition can shape the material conditions of societies, on 22 May 2015 after a long and protracted grassroots campaign, same-sex marriage was recognised as valid in Ireland via constitutional amendment (Dukelow and Considine, 2017). A similar story can be told in the context of contraceptive rights. Influenced by the Catholic Church, all forms of contraception were illegal in Ireland from 1935 until 1980. Again, this amounted to a non-recognition of the fact that persons should be able to make decisions about how they wished to plan their families. It was also a form of misrecognition in that there was a pervasive moral dimension as to why contraceptives were made illegal in the first place, the implication being that they would promote promiscuity. Yet, even if this latter point is reductionist and largely untrue, it is irrelevant in the context of people having the right to exercise their freedoms as they please where there is no harm to others. As was the case with same-sex marriage, recognition of the right to contraception came via grassroots campaigning coupled with increasing liberalisation (Dukelow and Considine, 2017). In both cases, people will have experienced being both misrecognised along with non-recognition.

Misrecognition and stigma

If we take the case of same-sex sexual activity, not only was this misrecognised but it was also deeply stigmatised. The same can be said for people who experience socioeconomic discrimination based on their class, what they wear or their accent. Not only are they misrecognised, but they are also stigmatised as a result of this misrecognition. Though they were engaged in very different projects, this is where the work of Goffman can be used to add a useful corollary to Honneth's work. Goffman (1990: 24) describes stigma types in the following terms:

> First there are abominations of the body – the various physical deformities. Next there are blemishes of individual character perceived as weak will, domineering or unnatural passions, treacherous or rigid beliefs, and dishonesty, these being inferred from a known record of, for example, mental disorder, imprisonment, addiction, homosexuality, unemployment, suicidal attempts, and radical political behaviour. Finally there are the tribal stigmas of race, nation, and religion, these being stigma that can be transmitted through lineages and equally contaminate all members of a family.

It is not hard to read misrecognition into what Goffman (1990) has presented here. For Goffman (1990), stigma exists in the nature of social relationships and not in the attribute itself. So, when he refers to someone with a 'mental disorder' or to someone as being stigmatised through race, he is effectively talking about forms of recognition and about misrecognition specifically. Goffman (1990) is not commenting on 'mental disorder' or on race in and of themselves. Rather he is saying that these are aspects of identity that are continually misrecognised, and they are stigmatised as a result. What is more, when people or aspects of identity are misrecognised and therefore stigmatised, this can cause people to feel the need to hide aspects of their identity, change their behaviour or engage in impression management, which can deeply affect them both personally and socially. However, these types of misrecognitions can be challenged and changed and as the examples given in the previous section show, what may once have been misrecognised and therefore stigmatised may, over time, gain recognition, often as a result of significant struggle.

Social work and misrecognition

When thinking about social work and the potential for misrecognition, it might be useful to think about this in two ways. The first of these is interpersonal misrecognition wherein a social worker fails to recognise a service user as a unique human individual or where an important aspect of a service user's identity is dismissed or overlooked. This could have obvious repercussions for relationship building and so guarding against misrecognition in this way can be an important thing for the social worker to consider. Conversely, the social worker deserves to be recognised as someone who has a mandate and who is working hard on behalf of the service user, even where views differ. The second type of misrecognition that might be useful when thinking about social work is institutional misrecognition. This is largely beyond the individual social worker and happens in the context of big institutions. It can take a number of forms and manifest in overly bureaucratic responses to human need, a lack of partnership or meaningful opportunity for service users to work in partnership or an emphasis on social control over and above social care. Where the opportunity to subvert institutional misrecognition comes back to the social worker lies in the ability of the social worker to reflect on whether or not the person they are working with has suffered from institutional misrecognition and thereby factoring this into assessment and response.

Summary

In this chapter we explored Axel Honneth's (1995) theory of recognition and related this to social work. We saw that for Honneth, recognition is channelled through the love that can be found in mutually affirming relationships, through respect that is conferred through the recognition of rights and through esteem that can be attained through opportunities to contribute to community or society. We saw that while these forms of recognition play out in everyday interactions, for Honneth they are the necessary building blocks for a fair and just society and so go beyond micro-personal interactions by having the potential to evoke substantive material change. We also saw that where recognition is possible, misrecognition and non-recognition can also occur and that this can have very real impacts for the people who experience them. However, we saw that rights and recognitions are something that can be fought for and obtained, thus changing the shape of society. In the context of social work, we noted that the people social workers work with may have experienced personal and institutional misrecognition. We also noted that social workers can strive to be aware of this and can be ready to offer recognition to those they work with.

For students: Exercise box 6

In this chapter we explored the work of Axel Honneth, concentrating on his theory of recognition. To further explore your understanding, consider the following:

1. Drawing on your own personal experience, think about what it feels like to be recognised through love, respect and esteem. Now think about what it feels like to be misrecognised. Write about how each kind of experience made you feel.
2. Think about recognition in general. Can you think of some groups in society who have found it hard to gain recognition and rights? Conversely, are there groups who have traditionally not had problems with recognition? How are resources distributed among these groups?
3. Think about recognition in the context of social work. Could or does social work potentially misrecognise people or groups? Sketch your answer as a reflection.

Further reading
- This book written by Nancy Fraser and Axel Honneth offers an excellent advanced primer on recognition theory and captures the key debates:
- Fraser, N. and Honneth, A. (2003) *Redistribution or Recognition? A Political–Philosophical Exchange*, London: Verso.

Why not watch!
There are many useful clips on YouTube that may help to flesh out and deepen your understanding. One which is particularly useful is called 'Axel Honneth's theory of recognition' and is published by PHILO–notes and is available here: https://youtu.be/gGW0oZp7x_s

Why not listen!
Podcasts are a great way to learn! The following podcast is part of the 'Insert Philosophy Here' series and covers recognition related to Axel Honneth and other theorists. It is available here: https://www.listennotes.com/podcasts/insert-philosophy/recognition-part-3-history-e0LPYywvfDS/

Chapter references

Dukelow, F. and Considine, M. (2017) *Irish Social Policy: A Critical Introduction*, 2nd edn, Bristol: Policy Press.

Fraser, N. and Honneth, A. (2003) *Redistribution or Recognition? A Political–Philosophical Exchange*, London: Verso.

Garrett, P.M. (2009). 'Recognizing the limitations of the political theory of recognition: Axel Honneth, Nancy Fraser and social work', *The British Journal of Social Work*, 40(5): 1517–33.

Goffman, E. (1990) *Stigma: Notes on the Management of Spoiled Identity*, London: Penguin.

Honneth, A. (1995) *The Struggle for Recognition: The Moral Grammar of Social Conflicts*, Cambridge: Polity Press.

Houston, S. and Dolan, P. (2008) 'Conceptualising child and family support: the contribution of Honneth's critical theory of recognition', *Children and Society*, 22(6): 458–69.

Houston, S. and Montgomery, L. (2017) 'Reflecting critically on contemporary social pathologies: Social work and the "good life"', *Critical and Radical Social Work*, 5(2): 181–96.

Howe, D. (1995) *Attachment Theory for Social Work Practice*, Basingstoke: Palgrave Macmillan, Basingstoke.

Howe, D. (2009) *A Brief Introduction to Social Work Theory*, Basingstoke: Palgrave Macmillan.

Jun, M. (2019) 'Stigma and shame attached to claiming social assistance benefits: understanding the detrimental impact on UK lone mothers' social relationships', *Journal of Family Studies*, 28(1): 199–215.

Leadbetter, M. (2002). 'Empowerment and advocacy', in R. Adams, L. Dominelli and M. Payne (eds) *Social Work: Themes, Issues and Critical Debates*, Basingstoke: Palgrave.

Marshall, T.H. (1950) *Citizenship and Social Class and Other Essays*, London: Cambridge University Press, pp 200–8.

Niemi, P. (2021). 'Recognition and the other in social work', *The British Journal of Social Work*, 51(7): 2802–18.

Szeintuch, S. (2022) 'Social love: the power of love in social work', *Australian Social Work*, 75(4): 471–82.

Webb, S. (2010) '(Re)Assembling the left: the politics of redistribution and recognition in social work', *The British Journal of Social Work*, 40(8): 2364–79.

Whelan, J. (2020) 'The roles of values and advocacy approaches in Irish social work practice: findings from an attitudinal survey of practising social workers', *Journal of Social Work Values and Ethics*, 17(2): 39–55.

For instructors: A set of slides that accompany this chapter can be accessed through the book webpage: https://policy.bristoluniversitypress.co.uk/critical-theory-for-social-work.

7

Pierre Bourdieu and social work

Biographical note

Pierre Bourdieu was born in Denguin (Pyrénées-Atlantiques), in southern France on 1 August 1930. His father was a postal worker, his mother a homemaker and also a postal worker. The fact that Bourdieu came from a humble background was something that impacted upon and informed his later work. A promising student, Bourdieu gained entrance to the prestigious École Normale Supérieure in Paris, where he studied philosophy alongside the French Marxist thinker, Louis Althusser. He was conscripted into the French Army in 1955 and he lectured in Algiers during the Algerian War of Independence. An anthropologist first and a sociologist later, Bourdieu also conducted fieldwork during this time by undertaking an ethnographic study into the conflict, which focused on the Kabyle peoples of the Berbers. From this came his first book, *Sociologie de L'Algérie*, published in French in 1958 and later translated to English and published as *The Algerians* (Bourdieu, 1962). His later work, *Outline of a Theory of Practice* (1972/2003) also drew heavily on his fieldwork in Algiers. Upon returning to France, he began a career as an academic culminating in the position of Chair of Sociology at the Collège de France. Bourdieu died of cancer on 23rd January 2002 aged 71. Throughout his years as an academic, Bourdieu was also a public intellectual who was highly outspoken and critical of the neoliberal agenda. Alongside those already mentioned, a key text by Bourdieu is *Distinction* (2004) which offers a detailed sociological report about the state of French culture, based upon the author's empirical research from 1963 until 1968. In the time since its publication, *Distinction* has undoubtedly been hugely influential and become a classic of sociology. A further key text worth mentioning for its relevance to social work is *The Weight of the World* (2002) which took aim the social injustices apparent in neoliberal societies. In his time, Bourdieu has taken influence from many quarters. However, alongside being a theorist, Bourdieu conducted empirical work through which to ground his theories as he sought to uncover how various aspects of the social world were continually reproduced. On this basis, Bourdieu is best situated as a thinker who, broadly, has much in common with traditional modernity.

Introduction

Pierre Bourdieu has undoubtedly been one of the most influential thinkers of the late 20th and early 21st centuries and his influence has spread far beyond the disciplines of anthropology and sociology to influence thought in many other academic areas including education, psychology, social policy and social work. With respect to social work, both Bourdieu's broad social theory and many of his discrete concepts have clear and immediate relevance, resulting in a flourishing vein of literature and one which continues to grow (see Garrett, 2007a, 2007b, 2009; Wiegmann, 2017; Brough, Kippax and Adkins, 2020; Houston and Swords, 2022; Wolniak and Houston, 2022 for just some examples). Moreover, Bourdieu is one of the few theorists covered in this volume who explicitly referred to social work in his books. Houston and Swords (2022: 1935), drawing on a number of others, make reference to this in the following terms:

> In the 'Weight of the World', for instance, he was sympathetic to the profession's plight under neoliberalism . . . Social workers were obligated, he recognised, to implement bureaucratic protocols (under the aegis of the 'right hand of the State'), and yet, still promote social justice (as directed by the 'left hand of the State'). Being placed in this antinomy, or contradictory position, they succumbed to a form of 'social suffering' or crisis that came with the 'bad faith' of compromised welfare principles.

As flagged in the biographical note, Bourdieu was both a theorist and a researcher. This combination has arguably imbued many of his concepts with a tangible quality that can be absent in the theoretical work of others. His ideas are recognisable; they make sense. They can be used to think something through but also as the basis for research or, in a social work context, as a way to think about, inform and potentially enhance practice. Indeed, Brough, Kippax and Adkins (2020: 513) have noted that:

> Bourdieu's work has developed a series of 'thinking tools' which emerged from his empirical investigations into a variety of questions.

In developing these tools, key questions for Bourdieu have been:

- How do power relations operate?
- What is the relationship between class and capital?
- What is the relationship between structure, culture and individual agency (choice and ability to act)?
- What is the relationship between taste, consumption and class?

There have of course been critiques of Bourdieu's work also. However, for the purposes of this chapter, these are left to one side and a selection of Bourdieu's conceptual or 'thinking tools' that are notable and applicable in the context of social work are introduced. Much of Bourdieu's work has been concerned with the dynamics of power in society and with how these are continually reproduced, and he developed a number of concepts that can help illuminate this. Moreover, his met sociological work has a basis in attempting to synthesis or reconcile the agency of individuals with the structuring forces of society. With these two points in mind as an important backdrop, the Bourdieusian concepts that will be introduced and described are as follows:

- Capital(s), these being:
  - Economic
  - Cultural
  - Social and ...
  - Symbolic
- Habitus
- Field

These concepts will be introduced in the given order, but they could easily be introduced in any order. This is because while they can be thought of in discrete terms, they are, in fact, key components of an overall picture so that capital is important in the context of field, habitus is important in the context of different capital types and so on. Because of Bourdieu's prolific output, this list is necessarily selective and there are many more aspects of his work that could easily have been included. In this respect, the materials at the end of this chapter will help the reader to pursue more of Bourdieu's work should they wish. This chapter will proceed by introducing and describing each concept in turn and in simple terms. As each concept is introduced it will be related to social work.

Capital(s)

Capital is a concept that is usually acquitted in economic terms. However, Bourdieu broadens what is meant by capital by breaking the concept into a number of constituent parts. Economic capital remains an important factor in reproducing social relations but for Bourdieu, though it may be a chief and underlying determinant, it is not on its own enough to explain how societies continually reproduce social structures and class relationships in a particular way. Before moving on to describe discrete forms of capital, it might be useful to think of capital in general as what a person or persons have or have access to, or, in the case of symbolic capital as will be seen, as what counts as legitimate.

Economic capital

Economic capital as a concept will seem obvious enough to readers. This is the type of capital that includes income, wealth, financial inheritance, monetary assets, property; in other words, what people own. As a standalone concept, economic capital has been used in various ways to measure factors of social exclusion or inequality. For example, income levels are used as a metric for measuring poverty and property ownership has historically been used to measure inequality. There has always been a strong correlation between low-income levels and experiences of poverty just as there is a strong correlation between property ownership and levels of relative affluence with those who own property tending to be generally more well off. Amounts of economic capital available to persons tells us something about how social relationships are reproduced; however, for Bourdieu, the undergirding nature of economic capital is equally important in the context of the access to other forms of capital it can grant.

Cultural capital

Cultural capital is perhaps less obvious on the surface than economic capital but no less important for Bourdieu. Cultural capital can include abilities of the mind and/ or body, it can include access to, understanding of or even ownership of cultural goods. Institutionalised cultural capital is to be found in things like professional qualifications. Of cultural capital, Wolniak and Houston (2022: 3–4) drawing on Bourdieu note that:

> Cultural capital is by far one of the most important and original aspects of the theory, and Bourdieu ... distinguishes three forms in which it exists: in the embodied state, that is, 'in the form of long-lasting dispositions of mind and body' (for example, a particular accent); as cultural goods (for instance, pictures, books, machines and so on); and in 'a form of objectification' (illustrated by academic qualifications). It should be emphasised that the embodied state of cultural capital is its fundamental expression, being an integral part of the person, and converts into habitus. Cultural capital is transmitted from parents to children, and the educational system intensifies the differences in the capital, as it favours and supports pupils from privileged social backgrounds. Thus, those with the 'right' accent and deportment are advantaged.

This passage by Wolniak and Houston (2022) captures the essence of cultural capital and there is a lot to unpack here. In the first instance, we can note that cultural capital takes three forms, each of which is important in its own right. Embodied cultural capital is just that, it is scripted onto on the body and can be heard in the way people talk or even seen in the way people walk. This embodied cultural capital is the 'fundamental expression' of cultural capital meaning that this is arguably where cultural capital is most important in the context of social relations. This latter point will become important when we encounter habitus further on. Cultural goods as a form of cultural capital denote the type of objects in which ideas about culture are congealed or solidified and these might include literature, art and so on. Cultural capital can also become solidified through things like professional or academic qualifications. Key to all of this is the question of what kinds of cultural capital persons both embody and have access to and what effect this embodiment or access can have in terms of reproducing social relationships. Cultural capital also speaks back to economic capital on the basis that persons with higher levels of economic capital may have higher degrees of access to the overall stock of cultural capital. Wolniak and Houston (2022) also note that cultural capital is likely to be generational and that those with access to the 'right' kinds of cultural capital are likely to be advantaged in a way that allows social relations to reproduce themselves in their favour. As an example of this, in *The Inheritors* Bourdieu and Passeron (1964) demonstrate that while French universities were ostensibly open to people of all backgrounds, working-class people were far less likely to go. Moreover, where working-class people did manage to go to universities, they generally tended to achieve lower or poor results based not on ability or direct forms of exclusion but on a lack of cultural capital. In other words, the cultural capital required to do well at university was generally not something that working-class people had sufficient exposure or access to and this prevented them from doing well. Bourdieu and Passeron (1964) identified cultural capital as being present in things like arts exhibitions, classical music and literature.

Social capital

Social capital may appear as a subtle but incredibly powerful form of capital. In essence, social capital is threaded through the resources that can accrue to persons based on their connections, the networks they move through or the groups they belong to. Social capital devolves on who you know and, moreover, who you know that can help you. It is important to note that there have been varying interpretations of what is meant by social capital and that these can have similarities on the surface while representing very different ideas in practice. For example, in *Bowling Alone*, **Robert Putnam** (2000) conceives of social capital in inherently positive terms. Drawing on the notion of civic virtue, Putnam (2000: 134) presents a vision of social capital in the context of building social networks wherein:

> The touchstone of social capital is the principle of generalised reciprocity – I'll do this for you now, without expecting anything immediately in return.

Robert Putnam (born 9 January 1941) is an American political scientist specialising in comparative politics. His most well-known work, *Bowling Alone*, about the collapse in civic, social, associational and political life in the United States, is frequently used as a key text in social work education in the context of community work.

In this way, for Putnam (2000), mutually beneficial social networks were developed. However, Putnam's (2000) project was very different to that of Bourdieu. For Bourdieu, social capital that is manifested through access to networks, and the soft resources of those networks in the form of things like introductions, recommendations, access to job opportunities, advancement or promotion, the ability to 'get ahead' perhaps literally with respect to waiting lists, services etc, has deep structuring tendencies and plays a major part in the reproduction of social relations.

Symbolic capital

Symbolic capital is not a capital in its own right, rather it takes the form of the legitimate expression of any of the other three types. Wiegmann (2017: 96), drawing closely on Bourdieu, describes symbolic capital in the following terms:

> symbolic capital is best understood as a trait of favourability, held by of any of the three primary forms when they are recognized by the majority or by individuals in power as legitimate.

Symbolic capital is often characterised by prestige, status or social standing. Symbolic economic capital may take the form of shares, financial capital, land or other property. Symbolic capital in the form of cultural capital might be something like being able to speak Latin, play the cello or have a deep understanding of art history. Symbolic capital in the form of social capital may mean belonging to prestigious private members clubs or attending a prestigious school or university. These examples are not exhaustive and are given here for illustrative purposes.

Before moving on to briefly think about the implications of Bourdieu's conceptualisation of multiple forms of capital in the context of social work, it should be noted that alongside being made up of the things that people may have or have access to, capital(s) for Bourdieu were not static categories. Firstly, though many forms of capital do remain stable over time (classical music, for example, attracts significant cultural capital and this is likely to remain the case) economic resources can become devalued, things can become more or less culturally significant, networks and connections can change or dissolve. Different forms of capital are likely to have more or less cachet in different settings and this will be explored more when we consider Bourdieu's conceptualisation of field. Moreover, there is competition for capital on the basis that on the one hand scarcity imbues capital with value, while on the other access to capital means access to considerable power.

Capital(s) and social work

For students and practitioners, one way to use the Bourdieu's ideas about capital could be to think about the forms of capital that different social work service users have access to. As a brief 'thought experiment', consider the following diagram represented in Figure 7.1.

Now, pick any identity from the diagram and think, in general terms, about the degrees and forms of capital to which that person is likely to have access. To work through the steps, let's take the primary school teacher. Ask yourself, to how much economic capital will a primary school teacher generally have access?

Figure 7.1: Identities and occupations

Who fits where and what capital(s) can they access?

Primary school teacher	Member of the Traveller Community	Long-distance lorry driver	Asylum seeker
Lawyer/Solicitor	Lone parent and unemployed	Woman who is long-term homeless	University professor
	CEO of a major bank	Telephone helpline worker (part-time, zero hour contract)	

Despite doing an important job, primary school teachers are not very well paid so this could be low while perhaps not being as low as others in the group such as the lone parent; lone parents we know are historically over-represented in poverty statistics. To how much cultural capital is the primary school teacher likely to have access? Primary school teachers are well-educated and will need to be generally well-read and knowledgeable to do a good job. A modest income and reasonable work hours may also allow some space to enjoy and consume cultural goods. The teacher may be less well off in terms of cultural capital than the lawyer/solicitor but more well off than the call centre worker in this context. In terms of social capital, the teacher is less likely to have access to powerful networks than the CEO of a major bank but may have better networks than the asylum seeker. Finally, working as a primary school teacher while poorly renumerated still has symbolic value and teachers are generally respected and recognised for doing an important job.

These examples are speculative of course but in the context of the social worker/ service user relationship it should be possible to take stock of what capital a service user has or has access to by asking questions like: 'What financial resources does the service user have?', 'What cultural resources do they have or have access to?', 'What networks can they access for support?', 'What standing do they have in their community?' These kinds of questions and the realities they unveil have the potential to inform and enhance practice.

Habitus

Having explored Bourdieu's theory of capital(s), we next move to briefly explore his theory of habitus. This is an extremely important component in Bourdieu's overall approach and, though he was not the first to use the term habitus, it has arguably become synonymous with Bourdieusian sociology in recent years at least. Having huge explanatory potential and wide-ranging applicability, it can also be a difficult or tricky concept to fully pin down and has many potential layers of meaning. On

> Friend to and collaborator with Bourdieu, **Loïc Wacquant** (born 1960) is a French sociologist and social anthropologist. His research interests include urban inequality, ghettoisation and the institutional punishment of poor and stigmatised populations.

the one hand, habitus has metatheoretical applications and can be thought of as an attempt by Bourdieu to synthesise human agency and social structure to take account of both the ability of persons to act and the confining and shaping nature of social structures. **Loïc Wacquant** (2005: 316), collaborator and friend of Bourdieu, describes habitus as being:

the way society becomes deposited in persons in the form of lasting dispositions, or trained capacities and structured propensities to think, feel and act in determinant ways, which then guide them.

In this way habitus can be thought of as the way in which social structures become internalised for or embodied within individuals, shaping and forming their dispositions in the context of how they think, act, walk, talk, as well as what they aspire to, what they hold to be true and so on. Habitus also allows individuals to make judgements based on past experience of how to act or, moreover, how they might be treated or received in a given situation. At the same time, Bourdieu arguably does not intend for this to be read as overly deterministic and so while an individual's habitus incorporates all that has been learned, people are not rendered static by it and retain the ability to act and to change it. Using the language of dispositions, Bourdieu (1984: 170) notes this in the following terms:

dispositions ... are both shaped by past events and structures, and ... shape current practices and structures and also, importantly ... condition our very perceptions of these.

So, in broad theoretical terms, habitus describes how individuals and social structures combine, thus bringing together agency and structure. Affirming this, Houston and Wolniak (2022: 3) note:

> **Anthony Giddens** (born 18 January 1938) is an English sociologist who has published prolifically over many years. Undoubtedly one of the most published sociologists and a feature on reading lists where sociology is taught throughout the world, he is currently a member of the British House of Lords.

It could be said that habitus is a bridge between agency and structure ... In this conceptualisation, the agent is never fully free to make a choice, nor fully determined by the existing structures.

There are shades here also of the structuration theory of **Anthony Giddens** (1984) in Bourdieu's habitus, which was also characterised by an attempt to address the classical sociological problem of the relationship between social structures and individuals. Ultimately, Giddens (1984) argued that social structures are not separate and distinct from individuals in an objective sense, rather they are reliant on human actions, within which people draw upon rules and resources. Yet this is ultimately very different from Bourdieu's notion of internalised social structures manifesting in sets of dispositions with the potential to confer more or less advantage depending on the setting. To this later point, alongside being an overarching structuring force, habitus plays out at the interpersonal level on the basis that one's habitus or one's set of dispositions can effectively be seen and reacted to. This may play out in what people wear, act like, walk like, etc, but also in what they aspire to and what kinds of things they consume in the context of cultural goods.

Habitus and social work

There are three ways in which it might be useful for social work students and professionals to think about habitus. The first of these devolves upon the idea of social workers having an understanding that the people they work with have to a large degree internalised their environment, which has deposited within them a way of being in the world. Wolniak and Houston (2022: 12) suggest that it could be argued that:

> people, including social workers, do not consider their habitus, class and whole social background seriously enough, thinking that actors are completely free in their choices – or that their thoughts and acts are free in the sense that they are not limited to their privilege or lack of it.

This suggests that social workers ought to think deeply about the habitus of the people they work with, taking into consideration the class background and experiences that may have shaped them. Connected to this, social workers can interrogate their own habitus, which may be very different from, and so may foster unfair expectations for, those they work with. The final way in which habitus can be a useful tool for the social worker is in the context of institutional habitus. Adding another layer to Bourdieu's notion of habitus, this suggests institutions and organisation themselves can develop ways of acting or dispositions that can have a very real impact on how the people who interact with them are treated or perceived. Remaining reflexive and thinking through the social worker/service user relationship using habitus in these ways can help to shape and enhance practice.

Field

The final concept to be introduced here is that of field. It will be briefly sketched in order to situate both capital and habitus. However, it is an important Bourdieusian concept in its own right. Simply put, a field can be thought of as a structured social space, a space in which there are rules, regulations, decision-making structures, perhaps a literature or professional associations. A field does not have to be thought of as geographically bounded although there may be some geography to it. Social work might be thought of as a field. It is a social space in which there are rules and decision-making structures; there is a social work literature. Social work is boundaried in that not everyone can just pick up and do it, it demands a recognised qualification. Wiegmann (2017: 95–96) notes that:

> Bourdieu described these social spaces in language similar to that of a war or game, with 'battlegrounds,' 'stakes,' 'rules of the game,' 'power relations,' 'common interests,' and 'trump cards'.

This is because for Bourdieu, fields are spaces in which people compete for different forms of capital. These are spaces where people with a 'feel for the game' are also more likely to succeed. Bourdieu refers to this idea of having a feel for the game as *doxa*, which can be described as having a practical sense of what it is possible to both do and not do in a given context.

Bring it all together: capital, habitus and field

To finally bring the Bourdieusian concepts discussed in this chapter together, we can use the analogy of a game of football to lay them out in simple terms:

Capital

Capital in the context of a game of football might be thought of as what the team and individuals bring to the game.

Habitus

Habitus in a game of football might be thought of as representing the internalised understanding of the game of football that the players possess.

The field

The field in a game of football might be thought of as presenting the rules, the regulations and the space in which competition takes place.

To finish with an empirical example of how Bourdieu's concepts can be brought together, we can turn our attention to the field of higher education. In Ireland, a study published in 2019 by the Higher Education Authority (HEA, 2019) demonstrated that in the first instance, people who come from wealthier backgrounds are more likely to go to college. It could be suggested that this comes down to economic capital purely, but cultural capital is also likely to be a feature as pursuing higher education is something that is passed down from parents to children as a cultural good. Moreover, the study confirms that students in high-end healthcare courses, such as medicine, as well as business, finance and engineering programmes, are the most likely to come from affluent backgrounds. Again, there are aspects of cultural capital here as entry into these kinds of programmes has high cultural value. Qualification in areas such as medicine also has a huge degree of symbolic capital attached. In a finding that immediately evokes a sense of social capital, the study also finds that students from wealthier backgrounds will immediately go on to earn significantly more than those from disadvantaged backgrounds. Bearing this out further, the study also shows that nine months after graduation the average student from an affluent background will be paid around 30 per cent more than one with the same qualification from a disadvantaged background. There are clear indications here of social dynamics and social relationships being channelled through and reproduced via access to economic, cultural and social capitals, which in turn demonstrates the empirical potential for Bourdieusian sociology.

Summary

In this chapter we introduced and explored the work of Pierre Bourdieu. In particular, we focused on his outline of the different forms of capital including economic, cultural, social and symbolic capital. We also explored Bourdieu's theories of habitus and field. Taking these three major components of Bourdieu's work together we explored how Bourdieusian sociology could be useful for thinking about social work. With respect to different forms of capital we explored how economic but also cultural and social capital could effectively function together to reproduce social relations. We saw how habitus for Bourdieu combines the power of social structure with the potential for agency. Finally, we explored the concept of field as a socially structured space with rules and regulations. Fields are also spaces in which different forms of capital are competed for and where having a 'feel for the game' can lead to success.

For students: Exercise box 7

In this chapter we explored the work of Pierre Bourdieu, concentrating on capital(s), habitus and field. To further explore your understanding, consider the following:

1. Drawing on your own personal experience, what forms of capital do you have access to? Go beyond economic capital to think about cultural and social capital. How could not having access to capital(s) affect social work service users?
2. Think about the concept of habitus. Think about your own habitus and the experiences you embody that make you who you are. Now think about meeting someone with a

completely different life trajectory to your own. Can our own habitus impact on how we meet and perceive people?

3. Think about field. What fields are you comfortable with and able to move through and understand? Try to link these experiences to capital(s) and habitus.

Further reading

- This book represents an accessible, edited collection and covers the key ideas and concepts of Pierre Bourdieu in detail.
- Grenfell, M. (2013) (ed) *Pierre Bourdieu: Key Concepts*, London: Routledge.

Why not watch!

There are many useful clips on YouTube that may help to flesh out and deepen your understanding. One which is particularly useful is called 'Bourdieu – simple explanation' and is published by Cheryl Reynolds and is available here: https://youtu.be/87BPL62wyyU

Why not listen!

Podcasts are a great way to learn! The following podcast is part of the BBC Sounds 'Thinking Allowed' collection and is called 'A special programme on Pierre Bourdieu'. It is available here: https://www.bbc.co.uk/programmes/b07gg1kb

Chapter references

Bourdieu, P. (1962) *The Algerians*, Boston: Beacon Press.

Bourdieu, P. (1972/2003) *Outline of a Theory of Practice*, Cambridge: Cambridge University Press.

Bourdieu, P. (1984). *Distinction: A Social Critique of the Judgement of Taste*, London: Routledge.

Bourdieu, P. (1986) 'The forms of capital', in J. Richardson (ed) *Handbook of Theory and Research for the Sociology of Education*, New York: Greenwood, pp 241–58.

Bourdieu, P. (2002) *The Weight of the World: Social Suffering in Contemporary Society*, Cambridge: Polity Press.

Bourdieu, P. (2004) *Distinction*, London: Routledge.

Bourdieu, P. and Passeron, J.C. (1964) *The Inheritors: French Students and Their Relation to Culture*, Chicago: University of Chicago Press.

Brough, M. Kippax, R. and Adkins, B. (2020) 'Navigating the politics and practice of social work research: with advice from Pierre Bourdieu', in C. Morley, P. Ablett, P. Noble and S. Cowden (eds) *The Routledge Handbook of Critical Pedagogies for Social Work*, London: Routledge, pp 512–22.

Garrett, P.M. (2007a) 'The relevance of Bourdieu for social work: a reflection on obstacles and omissions', *Journal of Social Work*, 7(3): 355–79.

Garrett, P.M. (2007b) 'Making social work more Bourdieusian: why the social professions should critically engage with the work of Pierre Bourdieu', *European Journal of Social Work*, 10(2): 225–43.

Garrett, P.M. (2009) 'Pierre Bourdieu', in M. Gray and S. Webb (eds) *Social Work Theories and Methods*, London: Sage, pp 33–42.

Giddens, A. (1984) *The Constitution of Society*, Cambridge: Polity Press.

Higher Education Authority (2019) *A Spatial & Socio-Economic Profile of Higher Education Institutions in Ireland Using Census Small Area Deprivation Index Scores Derived from Student Home Address Data, Academic Year 2017/18*, Dublin: Higher Education Authority.

Houston, S. and Swords, C. (2022) 'Responding to the 'Weight of the World': unveiling the 'feeling' Bourdieu in social work', *The British Journal of Social Work*, 52(4): 1934–51.

Putnam, R. (2000) *Bowling Alone: The Collapse and Revival of American Society*, New York: Simon and Schuster.

Wacquant, L. (2005) 'Habitus', in J. Becket and Z. Milan (eds) *International Encyclopedia of Economic Sociology*, London: Routledge, pp 315–19.

Wiegmann, W. (2017) 'Habitus, symbolic violence, and reflexivity: applying Bourdieu's theories to social work', *Social Service Review*, 44(4), 95–116.

Wolniak, M. and Houston, S. (2022). 'A sociologist in the field of social work: Pierre Bourdieu's theory and its relevance for social work practice', *Critical and Radical Social Work*, 11(2): 183–98.

For instructors: A set of slides that accompany this chapter can be accessed through the book webpage: https://policy.bristoluniversitypress.co.uk/critical-theory-for-social-work.

8

bell hooks and social work

Biographical note

Born Gloria Jean Watkins on 25 September 1952 in Hopkinsville, Kentucky, bell hooks was an author, educator, social theorist and social critic. Undoubtedly people are often struck by the pen name of bell hooks which she chose as a way to honour her mother, grandmother and maternal great-grandmother, Bell Blair Hooks, while also signalling a preference for her name to be written in lowercase letters as a means of symbolically focusing attention on the female legacies she wished to honour, on her work and ideas and away from herself. hooks's early educational experiences in a segregated and all Black school were empowering and transformative and she refers to this in her own work on teaching and education. As a child, she was also an avid reader, and this was something that continued throughout her life; her wide and eclectic reading having much influence on her work. After moving to a desegregated school and completing high school, a period during which she later wrote about becoming disillusioned with the experience of education, hooks went on to complete a BA in English at Stanford University, an MA in English at the University of Wisconsin-Madison before going on to take a PhD from the University of California, Los Angeles. hooks had a long career as an academic and educator, beginning in the University of South Carolina in 1976 and going on to teach at a range of universities through the 1980s and 1990s including University of California, Santa Cruz, San Francisco State University, Yale and City College of New York. Alongside being a prolific reader, hooks was a prolific author with a huge range of interests, publishing more than 30 books over the course of her career. For this reason, it is difficult to pin down key texts. However, in line with the concepts to be covered later in this chapter, her first major work *Ain't I a Woman? Black Women and Feminism* (1981), along with *Teaching Critical Thinking: Practical Wisdom* (2010) and *All About Love: New Visions* (2000) all represent excellent examples of hooks's work at different stages and with different areas of focus and each will be drawn upon here. In 2004, hooks joined Berea College as Distinguished Professor in Residence where she taught up until her death from liver failure on 15 December 2021 in Berea, Kentucky. As a theorist, hooks is difficult to place with confidence but is arguably most often thought of as a poststructural or postmodern theorist. However, given her focus on dismantling and critiquing things like feminism, class, race and education, on balance, hooks is perhaps most easily thought of as having presented a mixture between postmodern scholarship and traditional critical social theory. In her early work there are shades of Foucauldian-style genealogy and discourse analysis and in her later work she clearly emphasises an approach to theory and knowledge that problematises and deconstructs. However, there remains in her work also a strong resonance with traditional critical social theory as she seeks to find ways to lay bare the reality of social conditions and how these have been arrived at and continue to function. Because hooks, not unlike Habermas, might therefore be thought of as a 'theorist in-between' she is placed at this juncture of the book deliberately and before we begin to cover theorists who are very definitely to be thought of as postmodern in orientation.

Introduction

While never out of print and continually engaged with, the work of bell hooks has recently come back into sharp focus in the context of the **Black Lives Matter** and other global movements as people arguably grapple with and struggle to make sense of experiences of racism, the effects of capitalism and the potentials of feminism. In this respect, hooks's work offers an exceptional corpus of material through which to attempt to interrogate, interpret and understand many aspects of contemporary global society. Moreover, hooks's work is on the one hand focused, in the sense that she returned to many of the same themes across multiple volumes. Yet her work is also diverse in that she visited many different themes across the course of her career. Race, gender, class and how these intersect have been continual focal points in her work and feature in such works as *Ain't I a Woman? Black Women and Feminism* (1981), *Talking Back: Thinking Feminist, Thinking Black* (1989) and *Black Looks: Race and Representation* (1992) to name just a few. hooks has also written extensively about education and what it means to engage in critical education over a trilogy of books that include: *Teaching to Transgress: Education as the Practice of Freedom* (1994), *Teaching Community: A Pedagogy of Hope* (2003) and *Teaching Critical Thinking: Practical Wisdom* (2010). Moreover, hooks has also written extensively on the subject of love and community in *All About Love: New Visions* (2000), *Salvation: Black People and Love* (2001) and in *Communion: the Female Search for Love* (2002). This leaves out her work on masculinity, culture, poetry, writing, film, the arts, emotions and many other touchstones and areas of scholarship that hooks was interested in and wrote about throughout her life. As an author, hooks, though an academic, also wanted her work to be widely consumed and so wrote with general audiences in mind. A beautiful writer, in the spirit of dismantling hierarchy, this has meant that her work is largely accessible and readable. Further demonstrating her tendency to defy convention, much of hooks's work is not conventionally referenced in the way that most academic texts are. This is something that hooks has been criticised for both in the context of the scholarly attributes of her work and on the basis that her insistence on simple approaches denotes a

> **Black Lives Matter** is a political and social movement that seeks to highlight and challenge racism, discrimination and racial inequality experienced by Black people while also promoting anti-racist perspectives generally.

lack of respect for the sophistication of her audience. However, hooks did and would certainly still reject this criticism outright, favouring accessibility over and above academic convention regardless of the charge. One difficulty that can arise from hooks's unconventional approach to scholarship is that it is not always easy to detect or decipher who her influences were and so these have to be read into her work where they are not obvious or in direct quotation. However, the weight of her own thought and contribution more than makes up for this and in each area of scholarship hooks has turned her attention towards, she has offered profound contributions that stand up to critical scrutiny and offer abundant critical insights. Moreover, if critical theory remains concerned with unmasking modes of domination, then hooks, as a contemporary critical theorist, may be said to have been engaged in symbolically doing so by continually defying academic convention in how she presented her work. Key in much of hooks's work is her own biography, experiences and observations as a Black female author and academic, which she broadens out to the experiences of people in general so that, for example, in her work on education, she draws on her own experiences of the school and university system as a student and of the university system as a scholar and educator.

In the same way that the work of hooks offers much that can be useful in making sense of contemporary society, her work and the general ideas that she was concerned with can also be used to think about different facets of social work. In this respect, the concepts to be covered in this chapter include:

- Intersectionality
- Critical thinking
- Love and community

Each of these areas will be unpacked briefly and related in turn to social work. Limiting this chapter to just these three areas very much means that the surface of bell hooks's contribution is only lightly scratched here. In this respect, at the end of the chapter, additional materials will be flagged to help readers who wish to go further to deepen their understanding.

Intersectionality

Intersectionality as both a term and a mode of analytical and sociological practice does not start with hooks, though she arguably did much to popularise it. As we will have seen from our chapter on Du Bois where we referenced his work in *The Philadelphia Negro* (1899), intersectionality as an approach to theory building and which takes into consideration multiple and cumulative aspects of disadvantage and oppression has a long history in sociological practice even if it was not named as such. The term intersectionality was undoubtedly most famously coined by the pioneering scholar and writer on civil rights, critical race theory and Black feminist legal theory, Kimberlé W. Crenshaw, whose own work resonates in many ways with that of hooks.

In her 1989 essay, 'Demarginalizing the Intersection of Race and Sex: A Black Feminist Critique of Anti-Discrimination Doctrine Feminist Theory and Antiracist Politics', Crenshaw develops the concept of intersectionality as a way of demonstrating how both gender and race came together as dual tracks in the oppression of Black African-American women. Here she suggested that when discrimination based on the race and gender of Black African-American women were looked at in isolation from each other or along what she described as a 'single categorical axis', something is missed in the analysis. Crenshaw (1989) argued that when experienced together, oppression and discrimination based on both gender and race became compounded and as a result were much more potent and impactful than a single form of oppression. The tendency to separate the two was something she saw as deeply problematic, and she summed this up in the following terms with respect to Black women who were oppressed on the basis of both race and gender (1989: 140):

> Because the intersectional experience is greater than the sum of racism and sexism, any analysis that does not take intersectionality into account cannot sufficiently address the particular manner in which Black women are subordinated.

While Crenshaw's focus was very much on Black women in the context of legal proceedings, the value of this line of analysis can clearly be broadened to think sociologically about oppression and discrimination in all its forms and with respect to diverse cohorts. Indeed, Crenshaw (1989: 140) implicitly suggests this at the outset of her essay by noting that:

> With Black women as the starting point, it becomes more apparent how dominant conceptions of discrimination condition us to think about subordination as disadvantage occurring along a single categorical axis.

Here Crenshaw is suggesting that we tend to think about discrimination in general in singular terms. By moving away from such an approach, we can therefore analyse how different cohorts of oppressed or discriminated against people can face multiple forms of oppression and discrimination. From a social work perspective, a practice which approaches work with service users by considering the multiplicity of challenges they may face in their lives is likely to be more effective at identifying areas of concern and, therefore, at identifying actions that can be taken. Indeed, in setting out her stall for anti-oppressive social work practice, and referencing intersectionality directly, Tedam (2021: 12) notes that:

> the way in which the interconnections of social categories such as race, gender, age, ability and class create unique experiences of discrimination and oppression ... This results in situations where there is always more than one factor that can result in people being oppressed or discriminated against.

Intersectionality as a concept then has clear potential for helping us to think about social work and social work practice. Returning to hooks, it is worth considering how her work potentially deepens understandings and potential uses of intersectionality. Crenshaw, in her original essay on intersectionality (1989) makes reference to hook's work in *Ain't I a Woman? Black Women and Feminism* (1981) several times. Crenshaw also references **Sojourner Truth**, the civil rights activist from whom hooks took part of the title for her own early contribution and by whom hooks was also influenced as someone who pioneered an intersectional perspective by calling attention to the fact that the experience of being both Black and a woman had been obscured by the feminism of her day.

> **Sojourner Truth,** born Isabella Baumfree (c. 1797 to 26 November 1883) was an American abolitionist and civil rights activist. Her speech, usually referred to as 'Ain't I a Woman?' continues to inspire scholars and activists.

The feminism of that time was seemingly more concerned with White women's suffrage at the expense of taking any critical position on the emancipation of Black women, which was positioned as something of a distraction or perhaps even a threat. With this as a starting point, hooks begins her work in *Ain't I a Woman* by tracing this history in order to show how Black women had effectively been silenced and cut adrift from the feminist movement. She does this by first documenting the sexism and appalling sexual exploitation faced by Black women during slavery, who were not just Black slaves but were Black slaves and Black women, a doubly subordinated status, before moving to show how the conditions and practices faced by their historical antecedents still affected Black women in America at the time she was writing. She calls the tendency for practices begotten during slavery to continue after emancipation the 'continued exploitation of Black womanhood' and again shows how both Blackness and womanhood coalesced in the form of compounded disadvantage and oppression, manifesting in sexual exploitation, assault and rape, which Black women in America continued to experience despite emancipation (1981: 56):

> Sexual exploitation of black women undermined the morale of newly manumitted black people. For it seemed to them that if they could not change negative images of black womanhood they would never be able to uplift the race as a whole.

Like Crenshaw (1989), hooks takes what would later be termed an intersectional approach here by focusing on both race and gender. However, hooks does so in the context of a historical and genealogical approach by showing how the intersecting modes of oppression and disadvantage that affect the lives of Black women have come to have the character they do. This potentially deepens our understanding of the intersectionality of disadvantages and oppressions by not just showing that it happens but by also making the case for *why*. Moreover, as an analytical approach, hooks develops a method that can be extended beyond her area of focus so that it should be possible to both identify current multiple disadvantages as they are happening while also probing why this is the case in multiple contexts. This is an important point for hooks and in general as in order to begin to disrupt and dismantle discrimination and oppression in any area, it is essential to understand the contours of oppressive and discriminatory practices by understanding how they came to be.

Later in *Ain't I a Woman* (1981) hooks moves to show why such practices appear to still be socially tolerable to the point of continuing as part of the texture of Black female experience with apparent impunity. At this point, she introduces what is arguably one of her most well-known conceptual departures and something to which she consistently returned through her critique of patriarchy. She starts out by dispensing with the myth that patriarchal power was the domain of the privileged White male only by noting that (1981: 87):

> patriarchal power, the power men use to dominate women, is not just the privilege of upper and middle class white men, but the privilege of all men in our society regardless of their class and race.

In doing so she notes that Black male activists and leaders concerned with restoring their masculinity were just as likely to attempt to subjugate and oppress Black women on the basis on their gender as were their White male counterparts, again demonstrating how being both Black and a woman intersected to compound disadvantage. While hooks is lucid and scathing in her critique of patriarchal power structure and of an anaemic feminism, she also nuances this by suggesting that such societal arrangements hurt the oppressors as well as the oppressed (1981: 17):

> There can be no freedom for patriarchal men of all races as long as they advocate the subjugation of women. Absolute power for patriarchs is not freeing. The nature of fascism is such that it controls, limits and restricts leaders as well as the people fascists oppress.

Here hooks likens patriarchal power to fascism and appears to be suggesting that until all persons are free from oppression, both oppressors and oppressed, no person is free. This is a bold move by hooks which suggests that we can do and perhaps must do better. Moreover, this assertion makes clear that by approaching oppression and discrimination through an intersectional lens, alongside identifying how and why people are oppressed in multiple and cumulative ways, it may also be possible to challenge and change things with a view to a better society for everyone.

Intersectionality and social work

There are multiple ways in which intersectionality as a lens can be useful when thinking about social work. In the first instance, social work as a practical and applied profession often devolves upon modes of assessment. With this being the case, it should be possible to include an intersectional lens in the work that social workers do by taking account of the multiple challenges that social work service users can often face and by asking: are there multiple aspects of oppression, discrimination or disadvantage affecting a service user's life? For example, what would it mean if a service user was both Black and disabled? How might these aspects of identity intersect? Or, what if a young male service user is working-class, experiencing poverty and currently not in education or employment? Could these factors coalesce to make whatever challenges this particular service user is facing more challenging than if only one of these things were happening? Moreover, by considering multiple forms of discrimination together and not looking at these in isolation, is the quality of assessment enhanced? Might it also mean that there are multiple avenues for intervention in this case? Tedam (2021), referred to earlier in this chapter, offers a model of anti-oppressive practice that I have adapted below and that is primed towards an intersectional approach and can be referred to as the '4Ds-2Ps' model. The two Ps represent power and privilege. These underpin societal relations in general and therefore the social worker/service user relationship and so must be kept to the forefront of all social work interventions. The four Ds in the model stand for discuss, discover, decide, disrupt:

- **Discuss**: Discuss what has brought the service user to your service or provision:
  - use anti-oppressive language;
  - be fair and non-judgemental;
  - acknowledge your power and privilege; and
  - listen for oppression.
- **Discover**: Attempt to discover and identify the process or processes of oppression. The position of the social worker is key here too.
- **Decide**: Decide how you will approach the situation at hand. What will your course of action be? Remember to explore a range of options. Oppression is often down to a lack of choices. Understand and reflect on your power and privilege.
- **Disrupt**: The disruption stage of this intersectional model involves reaching decisions that ensure the service user is no longer oppressed or, at the very least, that you are not contributing to their oppression. The aim is to disrupt oppressive systems.

(Adapted from Tedam 2021)

Using the work of hooks to think deeply about oppression and discrimination along intersectional lines, coupled with a model like that offered by Tedam (2021), may allow social work practitioners and students to bring something of real value to the work that they do by helping to inform and deepen assessment. A further and more abstract way in which intersectionality can be useful in the context of social work is as a reflective tool. Whether by students reflecting on the profession they are getting ready to enter or practitioners already in the field, thinking through the work using intersectionality as a lens can lend depth to understanding and can help develop critically informed, reflective practice that moves beyond individual accounts of social issues to examine and explore multiple factors. This brings us to the next concept to be covered in this chapter in the form of critical thinking.

Critical thinking

Being able to think critically about society and about social work and social work practice is a key component of the discipline at multiple levels and is introduced in social work education and hopefully carried through practice. Indeed, part of the goal of this book is help readers think critically about social work using the work of theorists who have offered critical insights about different aspects of the social world. For this to be successful, it will need to be a shared endeavour and readers will need to approach the works covered with an open mind and a willingness to interrogate their own thoughts, opinions and assumptions. In many ways, this mirrors hooks's assertion that critical thinking in the classroom requires the full engagement of all who share the space. Over a trilogy of books (1993; 2003; 2010), hooks explored critical **pedagogical** approaches to education and much of her work in this domain can be usefully adapted to help us think about social work. Critical thinking must of course involve forms of critique and so, in the first instance, it is important to note that for hooks, critique as a practice is not necessarily about disagreement or tearing something down and can be as much about illuminating new understandings. This is evident in much of her written work where she engages with and critiques authors, film makers and others whose work she finds value in critiquing. This is an important point for students in particular, who often mistake criticism for critique. With this in mind, we might say that when we engage in critical thinking, we should consider the value of an argument, or a practice, a course of action or an aspect of society in its totality so that we can make judgements about what might be happening, what is of most importance and how things might be challenged, changed and improved. In her chapter on critical thinking in *Teaching Critical Thinking: Practical Wisdom* (2010: 7–8), hooks suggests that children are naturally predisposed to being critical thinkers:

> **Pedagogical/ pedagogy** refers to the theory and practice of learning and is commonly used to describe approaches to teaching.

> Children are organically predisposed to be critical thinkers. Across the boundaries of race, class, gender, and circumstance, children come into the world of wonder and language consumed with a desire for knowledge. Sometimes they are so eager for knowledge that they become relentless interrogators – demanding to know the who, what, when, where, and why of life.

As adults, hooks suggests that we may have lost our capacity to think critically and to question as we enter a world that values conformity and obedience over and above a desire to question and to learn. Thinking therefore becomes a chore and a thing to be dreaded (hooks, 2010). If we take this analysis at face value, it can be suggested that critical thinking and the ability to think critically is something that has to be relearned so that students entering a programme of study with a desire to be social workers or social scientists will have to work to reengage the critical minds they left behind in childhood. hooks (2010: 8) sums this up by suggesting that:

> Students do not become critical thinkers overnight. First, they must learn to embrace the joy and power of thinking itself.

In practice she (2010) suggests that this means that:

> critical thinking involves first discovering the who, what, when, where, and how of things – finding the answers to those eternal questions of the inquisitive child – and then utilizing that knowledge in a manner that enables you to determine what matters most.

Based on this definition of critical thinking, it is not hard to see how it is essential to social work and resonates with things like meaningful reflection and critical assessment.

Critical thinking and social work

Critical thinking for hooks then is clearly about keeping an open mind, considering all possibilities and seeking the best possible course of action. This immediately resonates with social work and with the social work assessment process in particular. hooks describes critical thinking as a form of radical openness and suggests that it is something that requires work and commitment so that we don't fall into the habit of process-based thinking. Engaging critical thinking and radical openness then will require work and effort on the part of the social work practitioner and is not something that can be maintained passively. Continuously entering into reflective thinking, thinking about theory and moving between this and practice can help with critical thinking and with shaping critically informed and reflexive practitioners. Moreover, open mindedness, openness to ideas and a willingness to hear multiple perspectives can also be something that social workers seek to foster in those they work with as a means of finding the best possible path forward, whatever the situation or scenario they are faced with. hooks (2010: 43) suggests that this is possible in the classroom by working together and fostering dialogue:

> Learning and talking together, we break with the notion that our experience of gaining knowledge is private, individualistic, and

competitive. By choosing and fostering dialogue, we engage mutually in a learning partnership.

There are clear implications for social work here and this approach to working with service users resonates with many social work values and practice theories.

A further way in which to potentially recruit critical thinking into social work practice is to use and foster imagination and creativity. In a social work practice that has become more and more procedural and process driven, this may present a challenge but it is nevertheless arguably essential and necessary that social workers resist the move towards what Habermas would have described as instrumental rationality and embrace critical thinking in the form of creative and imaginative practices (Flynn and Whelan 2024). Moreover, the critical use of imagination can be a powerful and emancipatory tool, something that hooks (2010: 61) was only too aware of:

> Imagination is one of the most powerful modes of resistance that oppressed and exploited folks can and do use. In traumatic circumstances, it is imagination that can provide a survival lifeline. Children survive abuse often through imagining a world where they will find safety.

With this in mind, when social workers engage in the critical thinking needed to be critical and reflexive practitioners, they can also use their critical imaginations to think about the work they do, the lives of the people they work with and the modes of intervention they deploy.

Love and community

The final areas to be considered in this chapter on hooks are the areas of love and community. As you will have seen from our chapter on Honneth, love can be a powerful form of recognition, can help to build esteem and is arguably essential to overall well-being. Moreover, we have also seen that there is a social work literature that engages directly with the idea of social love (Szeintuch, 2022). For hooks (2000: 87), love is a potentially transformative concept, and an ethic of love can underpin the very way in which society is organised so that:

> Culturally, all spheres of ... life −[sic] politics, religion, the workplace, domestic households, intimate relations should and could have as their foundation a love ethic.

Moreover, hooks argues that love can radically alter how we engage with one another so that an ethic of love 'presupposes that everyone has the right to be free, to live fully and well' (2000: 87) as a starting point. However, while hooks recognises and makes a strong case for love as an underlying principle for guiding social relations, she also recognises the challenges that such a societal reorientation represents. In the first instance, hooks is frustrated by the fact that love, though we perhaps understand it implicitly, has long lacked an adequate definition. Ultimately, influenced by **Morgan Scott Peck** and latterly, in further developing her thesis, by **Erich Fromm**, hooks settles on a perspective on love as something you *do*. Moreover, she distinctly categorises it as something you can and must actively choose to do and differentiates between love, which you must do consciously, and care, which you can do without loving. hooks acknowledges that this is different to suggestions that love is instinctual or inherent in human behaviour. However, the power in defining love as something people can choose to do presents itself through the very fact that people *can* choose to do it. Furthermore, hooks (2000: 5) separates love from other cognate emotions or states of being such as lust, sexual attraction or obsession, family relationships or romantic partnerships by leaving no room for discrepancy in how choosing to love would see people treat one another:

> **Erich Fromm** (23 March 1900 to 18 March 1980) was a German-American social psychologist, psychoanalyst, sociologist and philosopher. His early work in particular is rooted in a critical theoretical approach. **Morgan Scott Peck** (22 May 1936 to 25 September 2005) was an American psychiatrist and best-selling author who wrote the book *The Road Less Travelled*, published in 1978.

> When we understand love as the will to nurture our own and another's spiritual growth, it becomes clear that we cannot claim to love if we are hurtful and abusive. Love and abuse cannot coexist. Abuse and neglect are, by definition, the opposites of nurturance and care.

There is no equivocation here for hooks: when we choose to love, when we choose to nurture one another, we choose to love willingly, and we do so conscientiously. If this is in any way tempered or compromised by hurt, neglect or abuse, then, for hooks, this is not love. This is clearly a radical departure from accepted understandings of love wherein someone who is an abuser may also claim to love the person or persons he or she abuses. However, for hooks, if we are to move towards a true ethic of love, we must dispense with the idea that those who abuse us may also love us.

Having decided what love is and what an ethic of love requires, hooks acknowledges the deeply embedded and structural problems that make moving towards an ethic of love on a societal level challenging. She notes that people are cynical about love, that love may somehow be conflated with weakness, that under the domination and impact of patriarchal social relations and because of deeply embedded masculine scripts, embracing an ethic of love is challenging:

Society's collective fear of love must be faced if we are to lay claim to a love ethic that can inspire us and give us the courage to make necessary changes. (2000: 91)

> **Martin Luther King Junior** (1929–1968) was an American Baptist minister, activist and political philosopher. He was one of the most prominent leaders in the civil rights movement from 1955 until his assassination in 1968.

hooks, however, challenges all this by suggesting that choosing to love should be seen as heroic, not as a weakness and by suggesting that an ethic of love and inclusivity may represent a tonic to a divisive world, allowing us to turn away from stratified and competitive social relations. In doing so she takes inspiration from the Reverend **Martin Luther King Junior** as a 'prophet of love' and a deep thinker and social philosopher who was also a critic of capitalism, violence, alienation and exploitation and who saw love as the ultimate force binding us together. Ultimately, hooks (2000: 143) extends this analysis to the possibility of community based on love, a community wherein:

Enjoying the benefits of living and loving in community empowers us to meet strangers without fear and extend to them the gift of openness and recognition.

Taking a lead from hooks then, we might say that fostering community based on an ethic of love may allow us to nurture one another and care about one another's mutual well-being while recognising one another as individuals.

Love, community and social work

While not perhaps something that immediately springs to mind when thinking about social work, love as a conscientious undertaking as described by hooks offers much food for thought. Social workers often work with people facing extreme levels of hardship. Actively approaching the work through the prism of love and with a view to nurturing those whom social workers encounter represents a potentially transformative approach. Undoubtedly, this would be a difficult undertaking, particularly in instances where reciprocation is unlikely. Yet, for hooks, love is something we choose to do and so to choose to love even in the face of challenging circumstances represents a radical and potentially transformative act. Extending this thinking to the way we can live and enter our communities potentially deepens our bonds with one another. Moreover, actively centring love in how we shape and design our social and practice policies potentially allows us to move beyond individual encounters so that love becomes more deeply embedded in social work practice. Finally, in using a definition of love that leaves no room for abuse or abusive behaviour, social workers potentially equip themselves with the ability to challenge such occurrences where they encounter them.

Summary

In this chapter we introduced and explored some of the work of bell hooks covering three broad areas. In the first instance we saw that bell hooks has left an extensive and eclectic bibliography covering a wide range of topics throughout her career. With respect to intersectionality, we saw that in order to fully appreciate the oppression and discrimination people can face, it is necessary to take multiple intersecting factors into account. Drawing on hooks's early work, we saw how she used the example of Black women experiencing compounded oppression due to aspects of both race and gender to offer what would now be referred to as an intersectional analysis. Moreover, we saw how hooks traced the emergence of this mode of oppression from the history of Black female slaves to the time in which she was writing (published in 1981 though substantial portions were written earlier). From there we moved to explore some of hooks's work on critical thinking. We saw that critical thinking needs to be actively practised and involves remaining open minded, exploring all possible explanations and understandings and ultimately moving towards the best possible understanding or course of action. Finally, we examined the concept of love as explored by hooks. We saw that for hooks, love was something that persons needed to actively and conscientiously choose to do, that an ethic of love was underpinned by a desire to nurture one another and that love and forms of abuse could not coexist. We also saw that hooks believed an ethic of love could and should underpin all fundamental aspects of how societies are organised.

For students: Exercise box 8

In this chapter we explored the work of bell hooks, concentrating on intersectionality, critical thinking and love and community. To further explore your understanding, consider the following:

1. Drawing on your own personal experience, can you use intersectionality as a lens to explore challenges you may have faced?
2. Using hooks's ideas about critical thinking, what does it mean to be a critically informed social work practitioner and what would this look like in practice?
3. Thinking about love as a radical concept, reflect on the place of love in social work practice.

Further reading

- bell hooks has left an extensive and accessible bibliography and I would suggest engaging with the work of hooks directly if you wish to explore the areas covered here or her extensive range of interests. The two books noted below represent two that have not been drawn upon or otherwise mentioned here, either of which would also make excellent starting points:

• hooks, b. (2000) *Feminist Theory: From the Margin to the Centre*, London: Pluto.
• hooks, b. (2013) *Writing Beyond Race: Living Theory and Practice*, New York: Routledge.

Why not watch!

There are many useful clips on YouTube that may help to flesh out and deepen your understanding. One that is particularly useful is called: 'Feminism is for everybody: a guide to bell hooks' and is published by the Sisyphus 55 YouTube channel. It is available here: https://youtu.be/2e3khpPyMg4?si=x5pckOhUH B1QMohe

Why not listen!

Podcasts are a great way to learn! The following podcast is part of the 'Partially Examined Life' podcast series and is called 'Episode 139: bell hooks on racism/ sexism'. It is available here: https://partiallyexaminedlife.com/2016/05/09/ ep139-1-bell-hooks/

Chapter references

Crenshaw, K. (1989) 'Demarginalizing the intersection of race and sex: a Black feminist critique of antidiscrimination doctrine, feminist theory and antiracist politics', *University of Chicago Legal Forum*, 1989(1): 8.

Du Bois, W.E.B. (1899) *The Philadelphia Negro: A Social Study*, Philadelphia: University of Philadelphia.

Flynn, S. and Whelan, J. (2024) 'A sociological reading of statutory social work and Irish corporate governmentality: on the death of creativity', *British Journal of Social Work*, 54(1): 95–104.

hooks, b. (1981) *Ain't I a Woman? Black Women and Feminism*, Boston: South End Press.

hooks, b. (1989) *Talking Back: Thinking Feminist, Thinking Black*, Toronto: Between the Lines.

hooks, b. (1993) *Black Looks: Race and Representation*, Boston: South End Press.

hooks, b. (1994) *Teaching to Transgress: Education as the Practice of Freedom*, New York: Routledge.

hooks, b. (2000) *All About Love: New Visions*, New York: Harper Collins.

hooks, b. (2001) *Salvation: Black People and Love*, London: The Women's Press Ltd.

hooks, b. (2002) *Communion: the Female Search for Love*, New York: William Morrow.

hooks, b. (2003) *Teaching Community: A Pedagogy of Hope*, New York: Routledge.

hooks, b. (2010) *Teaching Critical Thinking: Practical Wisdom*, New York: Routledge.

Szeintuch, S. (2022) 'Social love: the power of love in social work', *Australian Social Work*, 75(4): 471–82.

Tedam, P. (2021) *Anti-Oppressive Social Work Practice*, London: Sage.

For instructors: A set of slides that accompany this chapter can be accessed through the book webpage: https://policy.bristoluniversitypress.co.uk/critical-theory-for-social-work.

9

Michel Foucault and social work

Biographical note

Michel Foucault was born on 15 October 1926 in Poitiers, France, into an upper-middle-class family. Foucault was educated at the Lycée Henri-IV, at the École Normale Supérieure, where he first became interested in philosophy. He later studied at the University of Paris Sorbonne, earning degrees in philosophy and psychology. Foucault did not immediately become an academic and worked for a time as a cultural diplomat abroad before he returned to France. Shortly after returning to France, he published his first major work, *The History of Madness* (1961/2006). Between 1960 and 1966 he worked at the University of Clermont-Ferrand, during which time he produced *The Birth of the Clinic* (2003/1963) and *The Order of Things* (1966/1973). From 1966 to 1968, he worked at the University of Tunis before again returning to France, where he took up the role of head of the philosophy department at the University of Paris VIII. Foucault next published *The Archaeology of Knowledge* (1972/1974), which expanded his method of analysis for uncovering alternative histories. In 1970, Foucault was admitted to the prestigious Collège de France. As is often the case in France, alongside being an academic, Foucault was also a public intellectual who offered opinions on and campaigned against racism, human rights abuses and poor prison conditions. Foucault's later work included *Discipline and Punish* (1975/1977) and *The History of Sexuality: Volume One* (1976), in which he further developed his archaeological and genealogical methods. Foucault died on 25 June 1984, at age 57, of complications from AIDS. Given his clear rejection of Enlightenment principles and his problematisation of things like truth and human nature, as a theorist, Foucault can undoubtedly be associated with the postmodernist tradition and in many ways represents an exemplar of the poststructuralist tradition.

Introduction

Michel Foucault was undoubtedly one of the major and most important intellectuals of the late 20th century. A divisive figure in the context of his intellectual contributions, which have been both welcomed and heavily critiqued, his work crosses boundaries and can be thought of as historical work, as philosophy and as social and political theory. His interests were wide-ranging, taking in explorations of literature, theories of power, histories of madness, prisons and the penal system, theories of knowledge, the body and sexuality to name just some. Irving (2009: 43) notes that:

There is an unmistakable shadow [and] theme of darkness, transgression and disruption that inhabits all Foucault's work.

> **Francisco José de Goya** y Lucientes (30 March 1746 to 16 April 1828) was a Spanish romantic painter. Donatien Alphonse François, **Marquis de Sade** (2 June 1740 to 2 December 1814), was a French writer, libertine, political activist and nobleman best known for his libertine novels and imprisonment for sex crimes, blasphemy and pornography.

This is undoubtedly true, and Foucault's work can be troubling and challenging to read, both in the context of the sometime density of Foucault's writing and with respect to what Foucault presents the reader with. This is arguably reflective of the fact that Foucault was himself an often deeply troubled person who had struggled with his own sexuality and with suicide and self-harm, particularly as an adolescent and young man. Foucault was also drawn to things that were dark and troubling: the art of **Goya**, the subversive literary works of **de Sade**, the philosophy of Nietzsche. These influences and others are threaded through his work. In many ways, Foucault can be thought of as an exemplar of anti-Enlightenment thinking. Taking a lead from Nietzsche, his body of work can be seen as a rejection of Enlightenment principles. Foucault rejects the idea that there are universal truths that are good for all times and in all places, rather there are 'regimes of truth' that are threaded through discourses and that are imbued with the power to shape, subjugate and discipline. He rejects the idea that there is such a thing as a fundamental human nature. Rather, for Foucault, people are made into or constructed as 'subjects' to be classified and categorised. There is clearly a huge challenge here for social work, which may be said to adhere to truths and beliefs about human nature in the context of care, confront and control, which are couched in the Enlightenment principles of the good, the beautiful and the true (Howe, 1994). However, there is also potentially huge value for social work in what Foucault has presented and his is a project that can be rendered in more positive terms. In this respect, Foucault notes that (1997: 325–6):

> I dream of a new age of curiosity. We have the technical means for it; the desire is there; the things to be known are infinite; the people who can employ themselves at this task exist. Why do we suffer? From too little: from the channels that are too narrow, skimpy, quasi-monopolistic, insufficient. There is no point in adopting a protectionist attitude, to prevent 'bad' information from invading and suffocating the 'good.' Rather, we must multiply the paths and the possibility of comings and goings.

This quote from Foucault (1997) speaks to the power of a questioning approach and challenges the reader to think broadly about the conditions of society at a given time. Taking up this challenge in a social work context might mean asking: why do the people encountered in social work suffer? Moreover, does social work have a role creating 'subjects' and perhaps thereby increasing or exacerbating suffering? Foucault's (1997) challenge also speaks to the possibility of multiple ways of knowing; ways of knowing that go beyond the often narrow sets of knowledges embedded in 'expertise'. Taking up this challenge in social work could mean allowing for a plurality of perspectives in ways that are both symbolic by allowing voices to be heard and emancipatory through potentially fostering partnership. At the very least, Foucault has given us a set of concepts that can be useful when thinking about social work. This is noted by Gilbert and Powell (2010: 4) who suggest that:

> social work can look to the work of Michel Foucault who provides an authentic 'conceptual toolkit' to interrogate power relationships between health and social care professions and service user groups.

With this in mind, the Foucauldian concepts that will be covered in the remainder of the chapter are as follows:

- Governmentality
  - Technologies of the self
- Discourse
- Power
  - Knowledge and power
  - Biopower
  - Panopticism and surveillance power
  - Microphysics of power

As the chapter proceeds, each concept will be briefly and simply outlined and related to social work. As will be seen, many of these concepts rely on and relate to each other so that bringing them together should equip readers with a decent grasp of Foucault's wider project. At the end of the chapter, additional materials will be flagged to help readers who wish to go further to deepen their understanding.

Governmentality

Governmentality is concerned with the activity of government in the formal sense. However, following Foucault (1972/1974), importantly, it can be suggested that ideas about government and about how and what to govern have shifted from a practice through which the activities of government were focused on political and civil life in the main to becoming much more concerned with the everyday lives of individuals. This suggests that governmentality can be thought of as being beyond the formal structures of the state so that we might say that governmentality is concerned with the 'art' of governing and with how people are governed in daily life contexts. Curran (2010: 807) notes that:

'Governmentality' refers to the proliferation of technologies to measure and manage the population as the dominant form of governance in the 'modern episteme'.

Irving (2009: 52), suggests that:

Governmentality for Foucault is both what we do to ourselves and what is done to us through all the techniques of bio-power.

If we take Curran's (2010) point first, for simplicity we can replace the word 'technologies' here with the word 'ideas' and this resonates with Foucault's notion of 'technologies of the self', which we will describe briefly further on. Taking Irving's (2009) assertion forward, we see that governmentality is also about 'what we do to ourselves'. We can suggest, therefore, that people can be governed through ideas as well as actions. Governmentality is often summarised as conducting conduct, an action on an action. For example, people are not forced to exercise, but instead are made aware of the benefits of doing so: you will be healthier, feel better, live longer, relieve your stress and anxiety (see Roche 2022: 51; also, Whelan, 2024). The acts, actions and discourses that make us aware, in effect, govern us.

Technologies of the self

A core feature of a more expansive conception of governmentality, technologies of the self refers to Foucault's (1988) concept of how people construct themselves and are in turn constructed as subjects to be moulded and improved in order to be better functioning members of society, whatever that may look like. For example, this may constitute a focus on self-formation or self-reflection perhaps achieved by improving diets, starting a fitness regime or drinking less alcohol. Conceptually, technologies of the self can mean that people are potentially self-governing though greatly influenced by the discourses that are transmitted by the multitudinous statutory and non-statutory bodies present in society at a given time. Technologies in this sense are, arguably, a core feature of neoliberal western societies (Foucault, 1988).

Governmentality, technologies of the self and social work

Taking forward the proposition that ideas can govern and that we can, and do, in effect govern ourselves through ideas, we can demonstrate this by thinking about what kinds of ideas govern in specific areas of life. So, for example, if we again take the area of physical and mental health and well-being, we can suggest that people are governmentalised through ideas about being healthy that suggest that we should eat right, exercise, sleep well, perhaps have a hobby. Readers are likely to recognise these ideas as those that they have encountered in various ways in the context of what it means to be healthy. Moreover, your conduct may have been affected by these ideas; many of us will strive to take these ideas up and try to be healthy. The more of us that do so, the better for governments with respect to things like health spending and medical care. For a further example, we might ask: what ideas govern the idea of being a good citizen? In answering we could suggest that to be good citizens we should work and contribute and shouldn't rely on social welfare or benefits. Again, you may have been directly affected by these ideas. Maybe you feel you should work, maybe you feel receiving a welfare payment is bad or maybe you know someone who feels this way and behaves in a way that reflects these beliefs.

Being governed by ideas such as these seems, on the surface, to be inherently positive; who wouldn't or doesn't want to be healthy or to be a good citizen? However, a difficulty emerges where people perhaps can't comply with what it means to be healthy or a good citizen. What if somebody can't work due to injury or illness, what if they can't exercise for the same reason? Given that ideas around things like work and healthy living are so pervasive, how will not being able to comply make people feel? How might they be treated socially or dealt with by the state? Social work governs its subjects with similar logics and with similar and different ideas. If we take the example of child protection social work, ideas about good citizenship form part of the social work brief but social work in this context also governs through ideas like 'being a good parent' or 'providing adequate care' or 'providing appropriate nourishment' or 'providing an environment for children to thrive in' and so on (Whelan, 2024). As with ideas about good health and good citizenship, these are all instinctively right and inherently good and desirable: of course we want children to be nourished and cared for. Yet, what can make ideas and governmentalising notions like these potentially 'irrational and ill-advised' (Roche, 2022: 52) is the lack of a grasp of the broader structural issues that those who come into contact with social work can often face and that can often be a real barrier to the realisation of all of these things (Whelan, 2024). This is because, whether subtle or overt, governmentality through ideas places the responsibility for realising the ideals that they describe firmly within persons. The implication for social work is that it may be necessary to think beyond the ideas through which social work governs, to take account of the broader environment that social work service users occupy.

Discourse

Closely connected to the concept of governmentality is Foucault's notion of discourse. Discourse is a hugely important Foucauldian concept and one that has since been taken up and used expansively by those that have taken influence from Foucault and those who have built upon his work. Powell and Khan (2012: 133) describe discourses 'as variable ways of specifying knowledge and truth'. Discourses are therefore powerful and effectively create and contain accepted branches of knowledges and ways of knowing that can deeply affect people's lives. For example, persons who are labelled as disabled are at once in the grip of a power and this includes power operated by professionals such as social workers or health professionals through their respective professional discourses (Powell and Khan, 2012). Drawing directly on Foucault (1972: 49), he describes discourses as 'practices that systematically form the objects of which they speak'. So, from this it can be suggested discourses and how we talk about or write about something, how something is 'discoursed', effectively brings that thing into being in the way it is described. Objects brought into being or formed in this way for Foucault included madness, punishment and sexuality 'each of which feature their own overlapping nexuses of power which guide, monitor, supervise, and regulate them' (Roche, 2022: 51). However, the same analysis could be applied liberally to many areas of life so that we could suggest that 'poverty' effectively comes into being through the way it is discoursed, 'unemployment' is thought of in the way that it is because of how it is discoursed and so on. When discourses are deeply ingrained, embedded and stable, they become what Foucault refers to as discursive formations, meaning that they confine what it's possible to say, think and experience (Irving, 2009). These kinds of embedded discourses will hold considerable power because they will characterise how things are responded to, so we will respond to poverty as a social problem on the basis of how we perceive it based on how it is discoursed. Discourses when powerfully embedded can also delegitimise, disrupt or render obsolete other discourses. For example, the discourse of science delegitimises the discourse of the supernatural, the discourse of medical science delegitimises the discourse of folk medicine or alternative therapies, the discourse of market economics delegitimises the discourse of collective redistributive welfare policy and state-sponsored services. A social work example may be how the discourse of managerialism delegitimises the emancipatory discourse of the profession (Powell and Khan, 2012).

It is important to note that Foucault does not suggest that discourses, powerful and entrenched through they may become, are immutable. Rather, Foucault leaves open a distinct possibility for challenge and change. Indeed, his method was, for the most part, about seeking freedom from the narrow confines of powerful and deeply embedded discourses and discursive formations that rendered other ways of knowing obsolete. In this respect, Irving (2009: 49) notes that:

> Foucault's archaeological and genealogical approaches have been a significant stimulus in taking us away from the notion that there is only one legitimate knowledge – scientific knowledge. Instead, he urges us to develop the capacity to unearth buried, suppressed and neglected knowledge that, historically, has been marginalized because of particular discursive power formations.

For Foucault then, it is possible to take any object of inquiry and explore it deeply to uncover how the object has come to be discoursed in the way that it is now and how it might have been historically discoursed. To take an example from Foucault's own work, in *Ethics: Subjectivity and Truth* (1997: 41–42), in recalling his work on the history of madness, Foucault notes the following:

> There is doubtless a historical correlation between two facts: before the eighteenth century, madness was not systematically interned; and it was considered essentially as a form of error or illusion. At the beginning of the Classical age, madness was still seen as belonging to the world's chimeras; it could live in the midst of them, and it didn't have to be separated from them until it took extreme or dangerous forms ... The practice of internment at the beginning of the nineteenth century coincides with the moment when madness is perceived less in relation to delusion than in relation to regular, normal behaviour; when it appears no longer as disturbed judgment but as a disorder in one's way of acting, of willing, of experiencing passions, of making decisions, and of being free.

In this passage we see Foucault's method at work, and we witness the possibilities for new ways of understanding what might seem like a familiar phenomenon. Foucault is telling us that yes, we see madness now in the context of the abnormal, as something to be locked away and medicalised, but it wasn't always so. Rather, mental illness is, at the current juncture, in the grip of a powerful discourse that shapes and confines, but this is something that is open to challenge and change.

Discourse and social work

The Foucauldian conceptualisation of discourse can be useful to help think about social work in a number of ways. Gilbert and Powell (2010: 5) note that:

> discourse produced within a network of disciplinary activities and embedded in social policy constructs social workers' experiences and their identities, as well as the experiences and identities of those with whom they interact.

Taking this assertion by Gilbert and Powell (2010) forward, of social work, we can ask questions like:

- Where is social work 'discoursed'?
- What types of discourses characterise social work?
- How does social work 'form its objects?'

Gilbert and Powell (2010) suggest that the social work identity is formed within social policy. It may also be formed within practice literatures such as codes of ethics, value statements and other documents that describe and prescribe practice. Moreover, social work is discoursed and shaped within educational settings where people come to be educated as social workers. In these various ways, social workers and thereby social work practice is formed. These same processes, alongside broader social discourses, also shape and contain the service users that social workers encounter in different ways. Think for a moment of numerous and various different social work practice contexts that there are and note that within these people will have been discoursed in various ways. If we take the example of disability, we can say at once that disability is discoursed in very specific ways, using specific language. Disabled persons are likely to be 'managed', 'categorised' and 'treated'. This might suggest that a person or persons with a disability is/

The **social model of disability**, developed most notably in the work of Mike Oliver (3 February 1945 to 2 March 2019), is based on the idea that it is not physical or cognitive impairment that disables persons, rather it is the social and physical environment that prevents people with impairments from taking a full part in society.

are in the grip of a powerful discourse that devolves upon the medical model of disability. This has real–life consequences and will affect how a disabled person or persons experiences the world. However, students of the **social model of disability** will know that there are alternative discourses of disability and that many disabled people reject absolutely the discourse that medicalises impairment. Moreover, social workers as professionals in their own right can potentially challenge dominant discourses and advocate with and alongside disabled people. In this way, the Foucauldian conceptualisation of discourse can be used to think about what the people social workers encounter are likely to experience based on how they are discoursed or how a part of their experience is discoursed and how this is likely to shape and confine the options that are open to them and the actions they can engage in. Therefore, as a thinking tool, discourses can reveal much while also potentially helping enhance practice.

Power

Foucault was a keen student of power and his perspective on power and the distribution of power was nuanced and complex. Social workers, as professionals with a high degree of power, can arguably take much from the Foucauldian conceptualisation of power. For Foucault, power was everywhere, wielded by everyone and a component of all social exchanges to one degree or another. Foucault also described different types of power and some of these will be sketched and related to social work below.

Knowledge and power

If discourses are the ways in which truths and knowledges are specified, power plays a major role too by making it possible for particular discourses to proliferate.

This is because power is constituted in and by discourses and legitimised over time. Professional power such as the power used by social workers is maintained and reinforced by the techniques professionals use and the questions they ask (Foucault, 1977). An analysis of power using a Foucauldian perspective must take account of how power is created, maintained and legitimised by examining the genealogy of existing power structures, by exploring how this power is distributed and by examining the methods (technologies and discourses) used to keep such power in place (Powell and Khan, 2012).

Biopower

Foucault (1997: 75) notes that:

> the endeavor, begun in the eighteenth century, to rationalize the problems presented to governmental practice by the phenomena characteristic of a group of living human beings constituted as a population: health, sanitation, birthrate, longevity, race ... We are aware of the expanding place these problems have occupied since the nineteenth century, and of the political and economic issues they have constituted up to the present day.

Biopower for Foucault then is quite literally power over the body or bodies, and he notes how this shift to biopower as a form of governance occurs in the eighteenth century. This is a very different and arguably more invasive type of power to the traditional types of power associated with states. In a striking example of biopower being exerted over persons in a way that is relevant to social work, Morris (2018), in her work on mothers who are at risk of having or who have had a child or children removed from their care via court order, notes the use of Long-Acting Reversible Contraceptives (LARCs) as prerequisite for entry to the 'Pause' programme. Of the mothers who wish to take part in the programme, Morris (2018: 820) notes that:

> It is a requirement that the women accept a Long Acting Reversible Contraceptive (LARC) in the form of a contraceptive implant for the 18 months they are part of the programme. They cannot access the well-funded resources without consenting to the LARC as this is deemed necessary to the 'success' of the project.

This example as given by Morris (2018) represents a stark illustration of biopower in action as the bodies of the women involved are very literally used to police entry to a government programme. Moreover, the women in question will not be given access to available resources unless they consent to a LARC, demonstrating how resources can be tightly controlled and distributed using biopower.

Power through surveillance

Foucault uses the analogy of disciplinary power that can be seen in philosopher **Jeremy Bentham's** plan for the 'optimal prison', the panopticon, as a heuristic for disciplinary power. To describe it, in this prison, every cell is inhabited by only one prisoner. In the middle there is a tower where a guard can be placed to monitor the prisoners. All prisoners can potentially be seen at all times and because the prisoners will never be able to know whether they are being watched or not, they will 'internalise' the disciplinary power and regulate their own behaviour as though they are being watched continuously. This construction also creates an individuality by separating prisoners from each other in the physical room. Of the panopticon, Foucault (1977: 11) notes:

> Jeremy Bentham
> (4 February 1747 to
> 6 June 1832) was
> a highly influential
> English philosopher,
> jurist and social
> reformer regarded
> as the founder of
> modern utilitarianism.

> The panoptic schema, without disappearing as such or losing any of its properties, was destined to spread throughout the social body; its vocation to become a generalised function.

In this way the panopticon described the proliferation of surveillance power through societies generally. In the context of social work, surveillance takes on multiple forms as social workers themselves are subject to professional surveillance and also engaged in the surveillance of social work service users. This makes surveillance power a powerful concept in the Foucauldian canon and one that social workers can use to both think through aspects of the profession and aspects of professional practice.

Microphysics of power

Foucault's conceptualisation of power suggests that it is a ubiquitous and pervasive social force, present in all social interaction. Gilbert and Powell (2010: 6) note that:

> whilst one social actor may exercise power interacting with other individuals, we also need to be aware that all other individuals also exercise 'power' in their social relationships often expressed through 'resistance' in its dance with surveillance.

Quite unlike traditional sociological interpretations of power wherein power is often monopolised by the state and/or other powerful groups, this suggests that all people have the potential to use power and to resist. In the context of resistance potentially being something that social workers should and can practice in partnership with social work service users, it could be suggested that in social work, power finds a space between top-down surveillance and bottom-up discretion. In this space, social workers can use what Foucault terms the 'microphysics of power' to resist surveillance and oppressive discourses.

Summary

This chapter explored the work of the French social theorist, Michel Foucault. Specifically, the chapter focused on Foucault's ideas about governmentality, discourses and power. We saw that as a theorist, Foucault followed Nietzsche by breaking with Enlightenment principles and favouring a perspective in which truths are rendered historically contingent. On governmentality, we saw that from a Foucauldian perspective, how people are governed is not always overt or obvious and can be subtle, relying on the proliferation of ideas. We saw that discourses are the ways in which truth and knowledge are specified. These can be powerful and can have a direct impact on persons by confining and shaping experience. Discourses can also be challenged and changed and much of Foucault's project has been concerned with exposing this possibility. Finally, we saw that Foucault's theory of power is nuanced and complex. Foucault suggested that power is pervasive and present in all social exchanges. For Foucault, power can also take many forms, both subtle and overt.

For students: Exercise box 9

In this chapter we explored the work of Michel Foucault, concentrating on governmentality, discourse and power. To further explore your understanding, consider the following:

1. Think about governmentality in the context of ideas that govern. Can you think of any pervasive and socially accepted ideas that have shaped your behaviour? What ideas are key to how social work functions?
2. Think about the power of discourses. Can you think of a discourse that was once dominant but has faded? Can you think of a discourse that remains powerful but could or should be challenged? What powerful discourses should or does social work challenge?
3. Foucault suggested that power is pervasive and present in all social interactions. How does power feature in the social worker/service user relationship?

Further reading
- This book is based on a series of lectures given by Foucault and is generally more accessible than other books written by Foucault.
- Foucault, Michel (1997) *Ethics: Subjectivity and Truth: The Essential Works of Michel Foucault, 1954–1984*, Volume 1. Paul Rabinow (ed). New York: New Press.

Why not watch!

There are many useful clips on YouTube that may help to flesh out and deepen your understanding. One that is particularly useful is called 'Philosophy – Michel Foucault' and is published by The School of Life YouTube channel. It is available here: https://youtu.be/BBJTeNTZtGU

Why not listen!

Podcasts are a great way to learn! The following podcast is part of the BBC Sounds 'Thinking Allowed' collection and is called 'Michel Foucault – a special programme on his work and influence'. It is available here: https://www.bbc.co.uk/programmes/b038hg73

Chapter references

Curran, T. (2010) 'Social work and disabled children's childhoods: a Foucauldian framework for practice transformation', *The British Journal of Social Work*, 40(3): 806–25.

Foucault, M. (1961/2006) *History of Madness*, London: Routledge.

Foucault, M. (1963/2003) *The Birth of the Clinic*, London: Routledge.

Foucault, M. (1966/1973) *The Order of Things: An Archaeology of the Human Sciences*, New York: Vintage Books.

Foucault, M. (1972) *The Archaeology of Knowledge and the Discourse on Language*, New York: Pantheon Books

Foucault, M. (1976/1978) *The History of Sexuality Volume 1: An Introduction*, New York: Vintage Books.

Foucault, M. (1977) *Discipline and Punish*, London: Allen Lane.

Foucault, M. (1988) 'Technologies of the self', in L. H. Martin et al (eds) *Technologies of the Self*, London: Tavistock, pp 16–49.

Foucault, Michel (1997) *Ethics: Subjectivity and Truth: The Essential Works of Michel Foucault, 1954–1984*, Volume 1, Paul Rabinow (ed), New York: New Press.

Gilbert, T. and Powell, J.L. (2010) 'Power and social work in the United Kingdom: a Foucauldian excursion', *Journal of Social Work*, 10(1): 3–22.

Howe, D. (1994) 'Modernity, postmodernity and social work', *British Journal of Social Work*, 24: 513–32.

Irving, A. (2009) Michel Foucault. in Gray, M. and Webb, S. (eds) *Social Work Theories and Methods*, London: Sage.

Morris, L. (2018) 'Haunted futures: the stigma of being a mother living apart from her child(ren) as a result of state-ordered court removal', *The Sociological Review*, 66(4): 816–31.

Powell, J. and Khan, H. (2012) 'Foucault, social theory and social work', *Romanian Sociology*, 10(1): 131–47.

Roche, Z. (2022) 'Life after debt: The governmentalities of debt relief', *Irish Journal of Sociology*, 30(1): 48–68.

Whelan, J. (2024) 'Governmentalizing the "social work subject": social work in Ireland in the era of corporate governance: A sociological analysis', in R. Baikady, et al (eds) *The Oxford Handbook of Power, Politics and Social Work*, New York: Oxford University Press, pp 775–91.

For instructors: A set of slides that accompany this chapter can be accessed through the book webpage: https://policy.bristoluniversitypress.co.uk/critical-theory-for-social-work.

10

Judith Butler and social work

Biographical note

Judith Butler was born on 24 February 1956 in Cleveland, Ohio. Attending Hebrew school as a child, over the years, Butler has indicated in interviews that they were interested in philosophy and ethics from a very early age. Butler studied philosophy at Yale University, where they received a doctorate in philosophy in 1984. As an academic, Butler taught at Wesleyan University, George Washington University and Johns Hopkins University before joining University of California, Berkeley. In 2002, Butler held the Spinoza Chair of Philosophy at the University of Amsterdam. Alongside being a theorist and an academic, Butler can also be described as an activist having served as the Chair of the Board of the International Gay and Lesbian Human Rights Commission as well as being active in the gay and lesbian rights, feminist and anti-war movements. Butler might also be said to be a public intellectual whose views have been sought and who has offered views on a range of issues including gay marriage and the wars in Iraq and Afghanistan and, more recently, the anti-gender movement and trans-exclusionary radical feminism along with the ongoing conflict in the Middle East. With respect to key texts, Butler is perhaps best known for *Gender Trouble: Feminism and the Subversion of Identity* (1990) and *Bodies That Matter: On the Discursive Limits of Sex* (1993), both of which challenge conventional notions of gender and develop a theory of gender performativity. Heavily influenced by a range of feminist thinkers, along with Nietzsche, Foucault and others, Butler's work comfortably sits in the tradition of poststructuralist or postmodern scholarship.

Introduction

As issues concerning gender and identity become more and more prominent in general social discourse and as this discourse in turn becomes more and more fraught and divisive, Judith Butler, particularly with respect to their work on gender, might be rightly considered one of the most important social theorists still active and working at the time of writing. Indeed, as societies begin to grapple with previously 'hidden away' along with new and emerging modes of identity and expression, Butler's work appears to be poised to offer many entry points into thinking about gender and biological sex, what these mean to us now, how they have come to mean these things and how this might, and perhaps should, be challenged and changed. With this in mind, while Butler's overarching project may be said to be one of disrupting, deconstructing or 'troubling' taken-for-granted categories, they are also concerned with emancipation. In this respect, while deconstruction forms part of their approach, Butler does not seek to replace taken-for-granted and relatively stable categories with others. Rather, drawing on broadly Foucauldian methods, Butler seeks to offer a genealogy of how such categories have come to appear immutable. Moreover, through doing so, Butler also seeks to expose the problematic and potentially oppressive and violent forms of social existence that seemingly fixed categories can create, particularly for those who find or feel themselves outside of taken-for-granted categories. For example, in critiquing feminism and questioning the category of 'women' Butler asks (1990: 7):

> To what extent does the category of women achieve stability and coherence only in the context of the heterosexual matrix?

Here Butler asks, how is our view of 'natural women' mediated by hetero-relational norms and what does this mean for feminism as a movement? This is a deeply troubling question for feminist thinkers as it calls into question the very category of women and the work that this category does in predominantly **heteronormative** contexts. Yet, it is also arguably a question with clear emancipatory potential and with an answer that suggests moving beyond narrow conceptualisations of women. Butler asks these uncomfortable questions by drawing on the work of other feminist theorists, some of whom will be visited briefly later. With some notable exceptions (for example, Featherstone and Green, 2009; Hicks, 2013; 2015 Rosdahl, 2020), Butler's work has perhaps not caught the social work imagination in the same ways that some of the other theorists visited here have.

> **Heteronormativity** suggests that heterosexuality is the natural or normal type of sexual orientation. It is underpinned by the idea of two genders: male and female.

Nevertheless, Butler's work has much to offer social work and provides ample thinking tools to help theorise different aspects of practice. Moreover, feminist thinking, thinking on gender and on how the relationship between social workers and social work services users can be influenced through how gender roles are traditionality or normatively perceived has clear implications for social work in the context of both theory and practice. In this way, Butler's work has often tacitly influenced social work. For this reason, though Butler has written on a broad range of topics, we will stick closely to their work on gender here before broadening it out to other areas. In the paragraphs to follow, and after detailing some of Butler's key feminist influences, the concepts covered to illustrate the usefulness of their contribution will include:

- Sex and gender and ...
- Performance and performativity

As the chapter proceeds, each concept will be briefly and simply outlined and related to social work. At the end of the chapter, additional materials will be flagged to help readers who wish to go further to deepen their understanding.

Key feminist influences

While Butler can certainly be thought of and identifies as a feminist scholar, they can't speak for feminism on their own and as such has had many key feminist influences. We have noted some of Butler's philosophical and theoretical influences in the form of Nietzsche and Foucault. Butler was also heavily influenced by critical psychologists such as **Freud** and **Lacan** who won't be covered in detail here but with whom readers may wish to familiarise themselves. However, because Butler's feminist thinking has been so radical, impactful and often controversial, it is worth sparing some words for some of their major influences in the feminist tradition.

> **Sigmund Freud** (6 May 1856 to 23 September 1939) was an Austrian neurologist who has generally been considered to have been the founding figure in psychoanalysis. **Jacques Marie Émile Lacan** was a French psychoanalyst and psychiatrist who was in turn influenced by Freud.

Simone de Beauvoir, The Second Sex

Simone de Beauvoir's feminist writings and particularly her work in *The Second Sex* was influential for Butler. In *The Second Sex* (1948), de Beauvoir suggests that men are seen as representative of what it means to be human whereas women are positioned as 'not men'; they represent sex itself. Women do not write, appear in or have a common history, and thus have no unique subject identity or position as a result. The task of feminism for de Beauvoir is to begin to imagine all of these things and to move away from a world in which women are subordinate to men, a position that benefits men greatly as they effectively profit from an inequality among the sexes. Writing in *The Second Sex*, de Beauvoir recognises the challenge that this project of reimagination faces and argues that women, or at least many women, have become complicit in their own subordination which can appear to confer some benefits and protection. Nevertheless, this prospect of reimagining roles and disrupting deeply embedded social structures was influential for Butler.

Luce Irigaray, Speculum of the Other Woman

Feminist theorist and scholar, Luce Irigaray was also influential to Butler's work. In particular, her work in *Speculum of the Other Woman* resonates with at least some of Butler's own project. In *Speculum of the Other Woman* (1974/1985) Irigaray suggests that women have been traditionally associated with matter and nature at the expense of a female subject position. This of course resonates with de Beauvoir's suggestion that women have traditionally been subordinated by being seen as 'not men'. Irigaray suggests that while women *can* become subjects, this is only possible when they assimilate to male subjectivity. In other words, a separate subject position for women does not exist and thus women are defined exclusively through their relationships with and to men. With this in mind, Irigaray's project as a branch of feminism has sought to uncover the absence of a female subject position, the relegation of all things feminine to nature/matter and, ultimately, the absence of true sexual difference in western culture in particular. As with de Beauvoir, Irigaray has been influential to Butler's own project which has been concerned, in part, with the expectations that can accrue to deeply embedded subject positions.

Monique Wittig, The Straight Mind

Radical in both thought and deed, in *The Straight Mind* (1978/1992), Monique Wittig interrogates heterosexuality as something that is not just a preferred sexual practice, but is, in fact, a political regime. In life, Wittig described herself as a radical lesbian and she and other lesbians during the early 1980s who were based in France and Quebec reached a consensus that 'radical lesbianism' ultimately posits heterosexuality as a political regime that must be overthrown. In grounding this argument, Wittig argued that lesbians are not women because to be a lesbian is to step outside of the heterosexual norm of women, as defined by men for men's ends and thus, towards the end of *The Straight Mind*, notes that:

> it would be incorrect to say that lesbians associate, make love, live with women, for 'woman' has meaning only in heterosexual systems of thought and heterosexual economic systems. Lesbians are not women. (1978/1992: 32)

There are clear resonances here with both de Beauvoir and Irigaray and, moreover, Butler's work which would come later also resonates with some of Wittig's ideas. In particular, Butler's concerns with apparently fixed or congealed identities and what it means to step outside of these, along with their focus on language and how this shapes reality and social expectations, appear to have some grounding in the feminism of Wittig.

Social constructionism suggests that characteristics typically thought to be immutable and based in biology, things like gender, class, race, etc are actually products of human definition and interpretation shaped by cultural, social and historical contexts.

Sex and gender

From about the 1950s and before many of the social movements – including feminist movements – that would categorise the 1960s came into being, sex and gender tended to be thought of in binary and biological terms; you were either male or you were female. The biological attributes and sexual characteristics associated with being either male or female effectively gave rise to a set of social expectations and prescribed social roles. Since the 1950s there has been more of a tendency to separate sex and gender, with sex effectively devolving on biology and gender being regarded as being **socially constructed**. The simple way to think about this is to say that this understanding sees sex as biologically fixed and fact-based and gender as potentially more fluid and subject to change. For example, the gender roles of both women and men in the 1950s have since shifted and changed in many liberal democracies in response to social movements like feminism and the gradual realisation of women's rights. A person born female in the 1950s will have inherited an assumed gender identity that would have expected her to marry a male partner, perhaps stay at home and assume the majority or, more likely, the totality of caring responsibilities. A person sexed as female at birth in the 1990s will have had to contend with a different set of gendered expectations; for example, work outside the home will have become much more acceptable by this time and same-sex relationships will also have become much more socially acceptable by this point, in liberal democracies at least. While Butler arguably does not do away with the notion of gender and sex as separate and distinct categories, Butler does problematise both and goes some way towards collapsing them into one another as being effectively one and the same thing or, at the very least, closely connected. So, for example, in *Gender Trouble* (1990: 7) Butler suggests that:

> If the immutable character of sex is contested, then perhaps this construct called 'sex' is as culturally constructed as gender, indeed perhaps it was already gender, with the consequence that the distinction between sex and gender turns out to be no distinction at all.

Butler bolsters this point by observing that masculine-associated gender characteristics tend to accrue to bodies that are sexed as male and feminine-associated gender characteristics tend to accrue to bodies sexed as female. This leads to a series of questions: if this is the case, then what is left to separate sex and gender? Moreover, how have sexed bodies come to be thought of in the way that they are now in the first place? Is one born a male or female or does one become one or the other and what are the repercussions and expectations associated with being identified as each? These are the types of questions that emerge from and are addressed within Butler's work. In beginning to answer these questions, Butler distinguishes between the 'doer' and the 'act' and draws on Nietzsche who, in his third essay from the *On the Genealogy of Morals* (1887/1990) wrote that:

> there is no 'being' behind the doing, effecting, becoming; 'the doer' is simply fabricated into the doing – the doing is everything.

In unpacking what Nietzsche is claiming here, effectively he suggests that 'acts' or perhaps more simply actions are what ultimately bring persons into being, there is no foundational person behind the act. In other words, the act comes first and the person second and not the other way around. Bringing this back to Butler and their work on gender, Butler uses this to suggest that gender and therefore biological sex are not simply fact-based entities residing in bodies that bring into being natural modes of expression. Rather they are constructed and made real in the doing of gender. For Butler then, we might say that gender is something you do, it is not something you are or something that is you (1990:25):

> there is no gender identity behind the expressions of gender; that identity is performatively constituted by the very 'expressions' that are said to be its results.

The Foucauldian conception of discourse that we explored in the chapter on Foucault becomes important for Butler here also with respect to what precisely 'imprints' social understandings upon bodies so that we might suggest that there is no correct gender and indeed sex is not a natural category either as it relies on discourse – how we talk about, write, teach about and otherwise portray gender and sex – to bring each into being. Moreover, there can be no 'natural' category of sex, biological or otherwise, without the language to describe it. Therefore, social scripts are inscribed upon the body and gender, sex and the characteristics associated with each are discoursed in particular ways that confer them with the quality of 'realness'. Butler (1990: 25) sums this up in the following terms:

> Gender is the repeated stylization of the body, a set of repeated acts within a highly rigid regulatory frame that congeal over time to produce the appearance of substance, of a natural sort of being. A political genealogy of gender ontologies, if it is successful, will deconstruct the substantive appearance of gender into its constitutive acts and locate and account for those acts within the compulsory frames set by the various forces that police the social appearance of gender.

In this passage, while firstly setting up gender as something you do, Butler also identifies their project as one which seeks to both disrupt and emancipate. If there is some difference between sex and gender to be gleaned from Butler's work, it might be found in the suggestion that sex is not prior to or independent of gender; rather, sex and gender depend on each other because sex is inscribed upon the body and gender is performative. Moreover, gender cannot exist without cultural acts that make it visible. For this reason, gender is ultimately unstable and performative, and bodies ultimately have no identity without the scripts, rehearsals, performances and acts of interpretation that confer it.

Gender and social work

Ultimately this analysis of gender can be taken up and applied to many areas of identity that have relevance for social work and for how practice is shaped. Sticking with gender for now, Butler's work can cause us to ask, what does it mean to label or otherwise see a person as 'woman' or 'man' and how will our expectations for that person be shaped as a result? Are we likely to treat a woman differently to a man? Are our expectations of each likely to be different? This line of questioning can be extended to take account of gender roles. So, for example, what do we expect from 'mother', and will this be different from what we expect from 'father'? How will this shape the social work assessment process? If we take a child protection scenario in which social workers become aware that a child is being neglected in the home, how might the social worker assigned to the case approach the mother of this child and is this likely to be shaped by deeply embedded and socially prescribed gender roles? Conversely, what expectations will the social worker have for the father of this child; will they be different? Through asking questions like these we can begin to illuminate Butler's concern for how social categories might have concerning discriminatory and exclusionary effects. Traditional gender roles for women in the context of motherhood will have historically been weighted with the expectation that mothers are nurturing and caring. Traditionally, fathers have been less visible as a directly involved or 'hands-on' parental figure within the home. These may seem like antiquated notions, yet they are deeply embedded and so likely to tacitly affect how we approach the social world and through this, social work assessments. In a case where a child is being neglected, the weight of blame may therefore fall implicitly or explicitly on a mother, suggesting mothers are 'policed' more closely than fathers. This speaks to Butler's (1990: 25) notion of 'the compulsory frames set by the various forces that police the social appearance of gender' but also goes beyond appearances to take in social practices. In fact, bodies that have been sexed as female and gendered as feminine have historically been policed much more closely than those sexed as male and gendered as masculine. For example, earlier we used Morris's work (2018) on mothers who were required to take LARCs as a prerequisite for entry to the 'Pause' programme as an example of Foucault's notion of biopower. Yet this can also be taken as an example of the policing of sexed and gendered bodies, and it is striking that there does not appear to be similar programmes for fathers who are at risk of having a child or children taken into care. While our focus so far has been on gender and on Butler's work on gender, this analysis can easily be broadened out to include other socially inscribed characteristics. It we take racialised persons as another example, we can ask a similar set of questions: what are our expectations of a Black person versus our expectations of a White person? What are our expectations of a Black mother and are these different from our expectations of a White mother? Are we likely to treat each differently due to how race has been inscribed upon racialised bodies? What about social class? Will we expect something different from a working-class or poor person than we would from a person from an affluent background? How will this manifest in how we approach each? How would it affect our judgement in the social work assessment process? This is not a perfect rendition of Butler's project, yet it demonstrates the usefulness of their work as a spur to deep reflection so that if a successful 'political genealogy of gender ontologies ... will deconstruct the substantive appearance of gender' (Butler, 1990: 25), a political genealogy of race might deconstruct and disrupt the substantive appearance of race, likewise social class, disability, mental illness and so on.

Performance and performativity

Performativity as given by Butler can seem like a difficult concept to grasp and is definitely hotly contested among those who have taken the concept up. In reality, however, it is more often misunderstood than not and that has had the effect of creating the confusion with which the concept is so often treated. The main source of confusion seems to lie in a tendency to conflate 'performative' with 'performance' and for Butler these are not at all the same things. In terms of the key differences, starting with the idea of what constitutes performance, there is a clear deliberateness here so that we might see performance as a form of imitation of what would be otherwise expected or seen as the norm. Moreover, such performances can be exaggerated. For example, Butler uses the example of drag artists who perform as uber-feminine, thus performing, while also perhaps reaffirming, gender expectations. While drag is clearly a performance and in this sense contrived, purposeful and deliberate, it does give us a window into Butler's concept of performativity in that it points to the fact that gender is effectively performed or 'done' even where deliberateness or consciousness is absent. In other words, drag artistry exaggerates the norms of gender performance and therefore drag queens enable us to recognise the imitation at the base of any structure of identity, and thus the absence of any authentic source. Gender then is a copy of a copy, not an ascription to something original. Again, evoking Nietzsche, the act is everything and effectively brings the doer into being. A further way in which Butler's conception of the performative is sometimes misunderstood comes via an understanding of performative as deliberate and cynical or insincere; for example, 'performative outrage' or what is sometimes referred to as 'virtue signalling' in which a person or persons seek to portray themselves as outraged over something perhaps for social cachet. This type of performativity, in as much as it can be called anything at all, should not be conflated with the performativity as given by Butler.

So, what does Butler claim for performativity and how is it different from performance? Sticking to the area of gender, we can start to answer by saying that performative or performativity for Butler means, in the first instance, 'acting as expected' based on the deeply embedded ways in which gender is discoursed. In other words, individuals acting or behaving in certain 'expected' ways that then have the effect of making gender real. This is not just a performance, rather this is not a performance in the contrived sense, this is a performance that is 'real' as specific understandings of gender have congealed over time. Moreover, gender in this instance is not simply a matter of choice on the part of the doer either. In this respect, in the preface to *Bodies That Matter* (1993: x), in clarifying their thinking on what they want to claim for the performative nature of gender, Butler notes that an understanding of gender as simply chosen or performed would indicate that:

> I thought that one woke in the morning, perused the closet or some more open space for the gender of choice, donned that gender for the day, and then restored the garment to its place at night.

This clearly would be at odds with a theory of gender performativity and as such is at odds with Butler's thinking wherein the doing of gender produces the person and not the other way around. Clarifying this, Butler (1993: x) notes that:

> performativity must be understood not as a singular or deliberate 'act,' but, rather, as the reiterative and citational practice by which discourse produces the effects that it names.

This again brings us back to the Butler's use of Nietzsche, who you will remember tells us that there is 'no being behind the doing'. To try to now place this in simple terms, we might say that it is the deeply embedded discourses surrounding gender that bring sexed bodies into being in particular ways and with the weight of particular expectations so that a person begins performing a gender identity without ever choosing, thinking or being conscious of it. This is performativity in action. Where this perhaps becomes problematic is when people don't easily fit into rigid regulatory frameworks that police gender and this is where the emancipatory ethos that lies at the core of Butler's project again reveals itself. To illustrate this, we can again work through a series of questions. So, for example, if we take a young trans person or a person who wishes to identify as gender fluid or non-binary, these modes of identity expression all fall outside of what are widely discoursed and generally accepted gender 'norms'. They are therefore seen as 'not normal' or perhaps even as wrong or, worse, deviant. In fact, diverse modes of gender expression create havoc in regulatory systems which were not created with diversity in mind. This has real and consequential repercussions for the young trans, gender fluid or non-binary person with respect to what each can expect from life, how they might expect to be treated and received, what they can access, where they should go for support or treatments, what they can dream of and whether or not they can reach their full potential.

We have stuck with the example of gender here, but one of the strengths of Butler's theory of performativity is that it can be used to interrogate any subject position so that it is possible to apply this analysis to diverse sets of social characteristics. For example, we might say race is performative and because of this, the contours of lived experience in the context of race are likely to be shaped and confined differently for a person racialised as Black or for a member of the Traveller community than they are for someone racialised as White. Again, this can manifest in how persons who are racialised in specific ways can expect to be treated and received, in where they can go and what they can do, in what they can access and in what they can dream and hope for. There are clear resonances here with Honneth's theory of recognition that we visited in Chapter 6 and Butler themself was concerned with the potential for misrecognition that deeply embedded discourses (which have the effect of prescribing what both is and isn't normal) can confer. In some ways, though coming from very different schools of thought, Butler's work might be seen as extending Honneth's work by offering an understanding for how forms of misrecognition can occur. Yet, through offering a theory of performativity as a means to understand and deconstruct, Butler also leaves open emancipatory possibilities. This is because it is precisely due to the fact that subject positions are performative that they can be challenged, can change and can shift. When they do, they change the nature of lived reality.

Performance, performativity and social work

There are many ways in which Butler's theory of performativity is relevant when thinking about social work. With respect to gender specifically, drawing on the work of Hicks (2015: 483), who himself draws on Butler, it is suggested that:

> social work processes involve the production of gender through practical means, which relate both to immediate, local, and wider, institutional contexts.

For Hicks (2015) gender is not merely something that resides within social work as a precursor to practice, social work processes in effect produce gender and because gender is performative, this comes with a set of expectations around gender roles. In other work, Hicks (2011; 2013) uses the example of assessing lesbian or gay couples as potential fosterers. Hicks (2013) suggests that there is an expectation in the assessment process that the applicants will uphold gender roles that are characterised by traditional views of gender. Based on this analysis, it is possible to suggest that there are distinct disadvantages for gay and lesbian couples who put themselves forward as potential fosterers and this devolves in part on how gender is performatively constituted in the social work process. This analysis by Hicks (2011; 2013; 2015) can be extended out and applied to multiple practice scenarios where gender and what is expected of gendered persons may have a hand in shaping how social work services users are received and treated. However, we can move beyond gender and beyond social work practice exclusively while still showing the usefulness of Butler's theory of performativity. In a study by Maglajlic, Sen and O' Stevens (2023), which looks at the diverse identities of both social work students and practitioners, the concept of performativity is tacitly present through the way in which those who took part in the study reported fears of potentially being mistreated or misrecognised for having modes of identity expression that fall outside of deeply embedded subject positions. The authors (2023: 2) offer a rationale for their study which suggests that it is relevant because 'more and more people identify in ways that fall outside of singular categories'. Despite drawing more firmly on Honneth and Fraser, the study nevertheless encounters or abducts aspects of Butler's performativity. In the first instance, it is notable and perhaps telling that despite issuing a call for research participants who hold what the authors describe as diverse identities and which requested responses from practitioners and students with dual heritage, multi-ethnic heritage, who were pansexual, bisexual or asexual and who were trans or non-binary:

more than half of the student (47 [56.6 per cent]) and practitioner survey responses (26 [61.9 per cent]) were filled out by cis, heterosexual, white women of single-ethnic heritage.

Moreover, the authors note that the comments left by respondents with this particular profile tended to 'query why the survey questions explored gender identities beyond a binary understanding, or employed the category of gender rather than sex' (2023: 9). This type of response to a survey covering the area of diverse identities, while not to be taken as unequivocal, is nevertheless indicative of the fact that the deeply embedded and performative nature of identities are seen as the 'norm'. Moreover, it shows how any perceived 'deviation' from the norm or indeed any action seen to be encouraging of such deviation can be deeply troubling for people and can come in for censure. Turning to the findings, there are multiple examples of respondents reporting feeling or being misrecognised and of engaging in impression management. Others reported such instances of misrecognition as having little or no effect. Yet, even in cases where respondents were not negatively affected, the very fact that their identities were continually forced into deeply embedded subject positions demonstrates the power of performativity with respect to expected and accepted identity types. Bringing this back to social work, Maglajlic, Sen and O' Stevens (2023: 14) suggest that:

> The fact that a number of students and practitioners holding minoritised identities voice experiences of misrecognition, discrimination and fears of discrimination in respect of these identities should give some pause for thought for the profession. The findings suggest that some social work learning and practice spaces continue to operate within heteronormative, white, European, cisgender norms.

This resonates strongly with Butler's theory of performativity, suggesting that deeply embedded ideas about gender, sexuality, race and ethnicity continue to underpin social work in different contexts.

Summary

This chapter explored the work of the philosopher, social theorist and activist, Judith Butler. Specifically, the chapter focused on Butler's work on gender and on performativity and related these to social work. We saw that as a theorist, Butler drew from many influences including Nietzsche and Foucault alongside many feminist theorists such as de Beauvoir, Irigaray and Wittig. We also saw that while Butler's project has been concerned to disrupt and deconstruct, it also contains clear emancipatory potential and is concerned with misrecognition and the injustice that this can create. On gender, we saw that Butler troubles both sex and gender as stable categories and argues that it is language and discourse that shapes the realities of these concepts and brings them into being so that sex is inscribed upon the body and gender is performative, it is something you do. We also saw that where people fall outside of deeply embedded gender categories and gender roles this can have real and tangible consequences. Moreover, we saw that this analysis can be applied to any subject position including race, social class, disability and others. We also examined Butler's theory of performativity and distinguished this from performance and from other understandings of performativity. We saw that for Butler, performativity is not a conscious undertaking but rather is the way in which deeply embedded discourses in effect shape the identities they describe and make them real.

For students: Exercise box 10

In this chapter we explored the work of Judith Butler, concentrating on gender, performativity and recognition. To further explore your understanding, consider the following:

1. Think about gender. How do you think society is gendered and gendering? How might gender shape the social work assessment process?
2. Reflect. Think about different subject positions; these might be based in things like social class, race, gender or disability. Which norms do you associate with the subject position you picked? Interrogate and reflect on how you would expect someone with the subject position you have chosen to act. What does this tell you about your own assumptions?

Further reading
- This book represents an accessible entry point into the work of Butler.
- Brady, A. and Schirato, T. (2010) *Understanding Judith Butler*, London: Sage.

Why not watch!
There are many useful clips on YouTube that may help to flesh out and deepen your understanding. One that is particularly useful is called 'Berkeley professor explains gender theory | Judith Butler' and is published by the Big Think YouTube channel. It is available here: https://youtu.be/UD9IOllUR4k?si=1poctBWTK-qBY0mu

Why not listen!
Podcasts are a great way to learn! The following four podcasts are part of the 'Partially Examined Life' programme and each episode proceeds through a discussion on Butler's work. The final episode includes an appearance by Judith Butler. The episodes are available here: https://partiallyexaminedlife.com/2020/02/03/ep235-1-butler-gender-trouble/

Chapter references
Butler, J. (1990/1999) *Gender Trouble: Feminism and the Subversion of Identity*, New York: Routledge.
Butler, J. (1993) *Bodies That Matter: On the Discursive Limits of 'Sex'*, London: Routledge.

de Beauvoir, S. (1948/1997) *The Second Sex*, London: Vintage Classics.

Featherstone, B. and Green, L. (2009) 'Judith Butler', in M. Gray and S. Webb (eds) *Social Work Theories and Methods*, London: Sage, pp 53–63.

Hicks S. (2011) *Lesbian, Gay and Queer Parenting: Families, Intimacies, Genealogies*, Basingstoke: Palgrave Macmillan.

Hicks S. (2013) 'Lesbian, gay, bisexual, and transgender parents and the question of gender', in A.E. Goldberg and K.R. Allen (eds) *LGBT-Parent Families: Innovations in Research and Implications for Practice*, New York: Springer, pp 149–62.

Hicks, S. (2015) 'Social work and gender: an argument for practical accounts', *Qualitative Social Work*, 14(4): 471–87.

Irigaray, L. (1974/1985) *Speculum of the Other Woman*, Ithaca: Cornell University Press.

Maglajlic, R.A., Sen, R. and Stevens, O. (2023) 'Beyond binaries? A call for improved understanding of diverse identities of social work students and practitioners', *Critical and Radical Social Work*, 12(2): 187–204.

Morris, L. (2018) 'Haunted futures: The stigma of being a mother living apart from her child(ren) as a result of state-ordered court removal', *The Sociological Review*, 66(4): 816–31.

Nietzsche, F. (1887/2008) *On the Genealogy of Morals*, Oxford: Oxford University Press.

Rosdahl, J. (2020) 'The panopticon effect: understanding gendered subjects of control through a reading of Judith Butler', in C. Morley, P. Ablett, P. Noble and S. Cowden (eds) *The Routledge Handbook of Critical Pedagogies for Social Work*, London: Routledge, pp 345–58.

Wittig, M. (1978/1992) *The Straight Mind and Other Essays*, Boston: Beacon Press.

For instructors: A set of slides that accompany this chapter can be accessed through the book webpage: https://policy.bristoluniversitypress.co.uk/critical-theory-for-social-work.

11

Giorgio Agamben and social work

Biographical note

Giorgio Agamben was born in Rome in 1942. Agamben studied law and philosophy at the University of Rome. In 1965, he completed a thesis on the political thought of Simone Weil, a French philosopher who was hugely influential for Agamben. Among other influences during his career were Martin Heidegger and Walter Benjamin, followed later by Michel Foucault (bio-politics), Carl Schmitt (the foundation of the state of law) and Hannah Arendt (totalitarianism). Something that is particularly interesting about Agamben's contributions is his tendency to be involved in projects outside of traditional philosophy and social theory. In this respect, Agamben has collaborated with film makers, writers and poets such as Pier Paolo Pasolini, Italo Calvino, Ingeborg Bachmann, Guy Debord, Jacques Derrida, Antonio Negri, Jean-François Lyotard and others. With respect to key texts, *Homo Sacer: Sovereign Power and Bare Life* (Agamben, 1998) represents Agamben's best-known work within the context of critical, social and political theory published in English. This publication marked the beginning of Agamben's Homo Sacer project, which he has continued in multiple volumes including: *State of Exception. Homo Sacer II, 1* (2003); *Stasis: Civil War as a Political Paradigm. Homo Sacer II, 2* (2015); *The Sacrament of Language: An Archaeology of the Oath. Homo Sacer II, 3* (2008); *The Kingdom and the Glory: For a Theological Genealogy of Economy and Government. Homo Sacer II, 4* (2007); *Opus Dei: An Archeology of Duty. Homo Sacer II, 5* (2013) *Remnants of Auschwitz: The Witness and the Archive. Homo Sacer III* (1998); *The Highest Poverty: Monastic Rules and Forms-of-Life. Homo Sacer IV, 1* (2013) and *The Use of Bodies. Homo Sacer IV, 2* (2016). Across his body of work, Agamben can be comfortably identified as a theorist working in the postmodern tradition.

Introduction

The last of our theorists, Agamben is perhaps less well known than many of the theorists covered so far, and this is certainly the case in social work circles. Despite this, Agamben has much to offer with respect to thinking about social work and his work from the beginning of the 21st century onward has become some of the most cited philosophical work in the world. Much like Butler in the previous chapter, Agamben is also someone whose work has taken on a new relevance in the context of recent global events and in particular the COVID-19 global pandemic and the various stages of lockdown this created. In this respect, drawing on his use of the concept of 'states of exception', which will be explained in detail further on, Agamben caused controversy for effectively criticising the global lockdown measures, which he saw as being replete with totalitarian tendencies, thus offering a view that was distinct from many of his contemporaries (see Agamben, 2020). In many ways, Agamben's contrary stance on the COVID-19-induced lockdown and other measures is indicative of the often-challenging nature of his work in general, which, while readily engaged with and recognised as important in recent years, was not always as accepted. From a social work perspective, Agamben's work is specifically challenging with respect to his perspectives on human rights, which he critiques as outdated and outmoded and, moreover, as potentially exclusionary and dangerous. Those studying or practising social work will know that human rights are often held to be a – if not the – major pillar of the profession at all levels. Therefore, considering the work of a theorist who effectively makes the claim that human rights are 'bad' is likely to be challenging to the whole of the profession. Take this up a level to where considering the work of Agamben means considering the work of a theorist who claims that human rights are not only 'bad' but that an unquestioned acceptance of human rights in western thinking has been disastrous and a veil for atrocity and abuse and the challenge becomes even more pronounced. However, social work also prides itself on reflection as a tool for improvement and so challenging even that which appears sacred and immutable should form part of a process in which social work, as a global profession, routinely engages. Agamben's critique of human rights can offer a useful starting point. Perhaps loosely belonging to a group of theorists referred to as the Italian School, Agamben can in many ways be seen as a successor to Foucault in that he has taken up and continued Foucault's project. Moreover, he pitches his first volume in the Homo Sacer project as being concerned with what he suggests was left unaddressed in Foucault's own project, namely the:

> hidden point of intersection between the juridico-institutional and the biopolitical models of power. (Agamben, 1998: 11)

What Agamben claims here is that while Foucault may have been concerned to scrutinise how people are both made subjects and concurrently objectified by governments, he failed to overtly address how these two things are potentially intimately related. This effectively becomes Agamben's starting point and the point from which his project of Homo Sacer proceeds. Although Foucault looms large, Agamben was not influenced by Foucault alone and draws on a diverse range of theorists in developing his own work, two of whom will be visited briefly in order to contextualise Agamben's offering. As noted earlier, Agamben has not really caught the social work imagination up until this point, with some notable exceptions (for example, Ottmann and Silva Brito, 2020; Whelan, 2024; Whelan and Flynn, 2023). However, his concepts have much to offer and can be used as thinking tools through which to theorise practice. In this respect, the concepts that will be covered in this chapter are:

- *Zoë, bios,* bare life and Homo Sacer
- State(s) of exception

As with previous chapters, each concept will be outlined and later related to social work. In this respect, Agamben's concepts are all taken together and 'stacked' as one builds into the next. The chapter will finish with a brief summary, an exercise box and signposting to further sources. Before moving on to introduce Agamben's concepts, it will be worth reviewing two figures whose work has been influential to Agamben's Homo Sacer project and whose ideas resultingly carry through Agamben's own ideas.

Simone Weil

Agamben's doctoral work scrutinised the philosophy of Simone Weil and as such, Weil's influence remains evident throughout Agamben's Homo Sacer project. In particular, Agamben takes up Weil's objection to the core ideas of human rights as a conceptual apparatus in which to ground philosophy. Weil's arguments concerning human rights are quite complex and often devolve on semantics to illustrate the insufficiency of human rights in thought, articulation and practice. In a well-known example of Weil's (1963: 21) argument, she offers the following thought experiment as a way to work through the problems with articulating things in human rights-based terms:

> If someone tries to browbeat a farmer to sell his eggs at a moderate price, the farmer can say:
> 'I have a right to keep my eggs if I don't get a good enough price'.
> But if a young girl is being forced into a brothel she will not talk about her rights. In such a situation the word would sound ludicrously inadequate. Thus it is that the social drama, which corresponds to the latter situation, is falsely assimilated, by the use of the word 'rights', to the former one. Thanks to this word, what should have been a cry of protest from the depths of the heart has been turned into a shrill nagging cry of claims and counterclaims, which is both impure and impractical.

So, what precisely is Weil trying to show here? In effect, she is using the above example to show that not only are there circumstances and situations in which violations against persons can happen on completely different spectrums but also that use of the language of human rights can be grossly ineffective and underwhelming where such violations are extreme and harmful. In other words, how can the 'right' of a person to withhold the sale of goods be potentially conflated with and spoken about in the same language as the right of a person not to be forced into prostitution? In the latter situation, Weil suggests that a much more grounded and personal language is needed to describe what is happening. Put another way, it may be pertinent to ask (Andrew, 1986: 76):

When we hear of human rights abuses do we think the language 'ludicrously inadequate' to represent injustices? Are murder and torture 'falsely assimilated' to the level of restrictions on mobility and rationing of food?

Weil argues that rights-based language is often employed thoughtlessly or even foolishly, which ultimately collapses the usefulness of such language into a very particular conception of liberal rights so that rights do not necessarily have any real connection to what may be thought of as moral, good or obligatory and so that arguments about what people 'have a right to' versus 'what it is right for people to have' become conflated even though the former may be thought of as aspirational and the latter obligational or even existential. Ultimately, Weil challenges human rights-based discourses as potentially obfuscating and even permitting abuses in a number of spheres. As a general example, we might suggest that in any number of global conflicts one side may invade territory, capture, detain and even kill persons on the basis of upholding human rights, perhaps the human rights of the invading force which it has deemed to have been threatened or violated in some way, perhaps the human rights of a group or groups in the invaded territory who the invading force seeks to 'liberate'. Effectively, this example suggests that the capacity to commit atrocities under the veil of human rights aptly demonstrates their fallibility. For Agamben, Weil's arguments about the limitations of human rights are crucial and are used throughout his own work.

> Perhaps most famous for his work *Leviathan*, **Thomas Hobbes** (1588–1679) was an English philosopher and social theorist. In *Leviathan*, Hobbes offers a social contract-based theory in which he suggests that it is best to be ruled over by even a tyrannical ruler than to have a situation where there is no sovereign power and in which a state of nature characterised by perpetual war exists.

Carl Schmitt

In his Homo Sacer project, Agamben elucidates the concept of 'state of exception', giving many examples and drawing on the work of political theorist Carl Schmitt.[1] In *Political Theology*, Schmitt opens with perhaps his most quoted line, 'Sovereign is he who decides on the exception'. Philosophically, Schmitt (1985: 36) follows **Thomas Hobbes** here generally by noting that:

---

[1] It is not the intention here to add to any 'rehabilitation' of Schmitt. In this respect, it should be noted for context that Schmitt was a committed member of the Nazi party which he joined in 1933. Moreover, after spending some time in an internment camp after he was captured by American forces in 1945, he returned to his home of Plettenburg where he remained unrepentant about his role in the Nazi state apparatus. His concept of the 'state of exception', on which Agamben draws, was developed a full ten years before the Nazi takeover of Germany in 1933 and so in using Schmitt, the man must be separated from the theorist.

All significant concepts of the modern theory of the state are secularized theological concepts not only because of their historical development – in which they were transferred from theology to the theory of the state, whereby, for example, the omnipotent God became the omnipotent lawgiver – but also because of their systematic structure, the recognition of which is necessary for a sociological consideration of these concepts. The exception in jurisprudence is analogous to the miracle in theology.

So, having suggested that the secular state in effect mirrors – theoretically and conceptually – the theological, Schmitt likens the 'miracle', a theological concept which perhaps creates new conditions for faith after which things will never be the same, to the 'exception'. But just what does Schmitt mean by the exception or by the 'state of exception'? In simple terms, a state of exception could include any major societal upheaval; for example, economic or political upheaval that requires the application of extraordinary and far-reaching measures. Schmitt's critique in *Political Theology* was concerned to show how constitutional democracies could in effect dispense with their own rules at times that suited and while this informs Agamben, he takes a different approach. Thinking of recent history (at the time of writing), we might also include in this a major public health crisis such as a global pandemic as a state of exception. While there may be criteria for confronting such crises, what can emerge from them can ultimately be of a new order. What is key here and what has been key to Agamben's project is the question of 'who decides' the exception and, moreover, on what basis. If we take the example of the COVID-19 global pandemic, this very much falls into the category of a state of exception as given by Agamben; it created major social upheaval, laws were suspended or changed overnight, emergency powers were enacted by many governments and people were severely curtailed in where they could go and what they could do to prevent the spread of the Sars-CoV2 virus. This state of exception may have been created for a series of very good reasons. However, for Agamben, influenced here by Schmitt, even the ability of a state to create states of exception is dangerous and totalitarian. In the paragraphs to follow we will interrogate why Agamben believes this to be the case. For now, we can note that this understanding as given by Schmitt is key to understanding Agamben's own work.

Zoë, *bios*, bare life and Homo Sacer

In starting his Homo Sacer project, Agamben (1998: 9) wants to distinguish between different forms of life in order to begin to show what's at stake when one or the other is threatened or when states of exception are created. He does this firstly by evoking the Greeks and the philosophy of **Aristotle** in particular.

Along with his forbears, Plato and Socrates, **Aristotle** represents one the most famous and influential philosophers to have ever lived. His work covered a range of topics including the natural sciences, philosophy, linguistics, economics, politics, psychology and the arts.

> The Greeks had no single term to express what we mean by the word
> 'life.' They used two terms that, although traceable to a common
> etymological root, are semantically and morphologically distinct: zoē,
> which expressed the simple fact of living common to all living beings
> (animals, men, or gods), and bios, which indicated the form or way of
> living proper to an individual or a group.

Here Agamben uses the Greek understanding of life as consisting of two distinct categories. *Zoë* is clearly intended to denote simple or pure life; it might also be thought of as animal life as encapsulated in shared human and, indeed, animal characteristics: the need to eat, to reproduce, to excrete, to sleep and so on. Placed more firmly in the human sphere, *zoë* might also be taken up to mean home life or domestic life. What is key here is that *zoë* as a kind or type of life is not political life; it exists outside of politics or at least it did in the time of ancient Greece and in the example that Agamben draws upon. For that other form of life, the type of life which is political, Agamben draws on the Greek understanding of *bios*. Separate from *zoë* but still fully part of what it is to be human and, indeed, a distinguishing feature of humanity, *bios* is the legitimised form of social life wherein political life resides. This is where political, civil, social and economic activities happen. So, for example, the right to vote or to free assembly or to belong to groups or to run for election are all aspects of *bios*. It can be useful to think of *zoë* and *bios* as being mutually dependent aspects of life in this example, one in effect relying on the other. For Agamben, the purpose of separating and rendering distinct these two aspects of human life is to begin the task of showing what happens when persons are stripped of either, but in particular when they are stripped of their *bios*, their political life. This is where we encounter the concept of 'bare life'. For Agamben, bare life in this instance, though similar, is not fully the same as *zoë* due to the fact that *zoë* can rely for its existence on the *bios* of persons. Moreover, it is possible for persons to exist primarily as *zoë* while not being forcibly reduced to bare life; for example women, children and disabled persons will have been seen as belonging to *zoë* in the Greek understanding that Agamben uses as having no political life while still not existing as bare life in a way that makes them Homo Sacer. This is because force is required to reduce a person to bare life in a way that renders them as Homo Sacer, meaning that when a person's *bios* is removed, when their political life is rendered moot, what is left is a shunned or banished form of bare life. Bare life in this instance is animal life in the truest sense as a person without *bios* and who has been reduced to bare life in this way has no more status than any other non-human animal.

Before moving on to discuss Agamben's usage of the concept of Homo Sacer, it is important to note that the *zoë*/*bios* distinction that Agamben attributes to the Greeks later sees the two distinct concepts become conflated and intertwined, particularly through the onset of modernity, the rise of the nation state and the emergence of biology as a science. For Agamben, rooted in biology in particular, this has the effect of locating *zoë*, that which had previously been seen as separate to political life, firmly in the domain of the political as governments begin to measure and manage 'bodies', ushering in what Agamben describes as biopolitics. There is obvious and overarching familiarity with Foucault's rendition of biopower here, which we covered in Chapter 9. In this new conflation of *zoë* and *bios*, Agamben suggests that citizens are rendered as objects but with political rights, which also makes them subjects and this for Agamben is quite distinct from previous periods in history while also representing a gap in Foucault's own project (who he suggests failed to overtly examine the two together).

Through all this, what Agamben is doing is developing his conceptual tools and building towards his theory of a state of exception by first demonstrating what it means to remove an aspect of a person's humanity and forcibly render them as bare life. In doing so, he likens the figure forcibly reduced to bare life to the historical figure of Homo Sacer. Homo Sacer is a figure of Roman law: a person who is banned and might, or might not, be killed by anybody but must not be sacrificed in a religious ritual. Homo Sacer or the 'sacred or accursed man' is therefore a person stripped of all political life (*bios*) and *forcibly* reduced to bare life (*zoë*). The fact that Homo Sacer cannot be sacrificed or used in ritual denotes a demotion to the status of animal. Likewise, the fact that Homo Sacer can be killed with impunity denotes that all political life has been removed from this person. Bringing all this together, Ottmann and Silva Brito (2020: 226) sum this up in the following way:

> Agamben differentiates between the socio-political persona and the biological persona. Bare life, in Agamben's work, refers to the person that has been stripped of all of her political and social status; it refers to the characteristics of a non-person, someone who has been reduced to her biological persona. People reduced to bare life are without any social or political protection. Their life is terrifyingly fragile as they can be killed without punishment; yet, because of its fragility, bare life is metaphysically regarded as sacred.

The sacred in the bare life distinction that makes Homo Sacer what it is can be confusing and should not be conflated with the modern usage of the term. Rather sacred should be thought of as meaning life as given by God or what is left when all else is rendered moot. It can also be thought of as life that exists outside of society or outside of the world of people. For Agamben, the major underlying concern in all of this is to show how democratic states tend towards totalitarianism by creating states of exception; by creating Homo Sacer. In extreme instances, rendering someone as Homo Sacer effectively renders them as a 'killable body' and, accordingly, rendering groups of people as Homo Sacer renders them as 'killable bodies'. Yet, for Agamben, this does not happen by accident but rather by design and when a state of exception is created.

States of exception

In sketching out what is meant by a state of exception, Schmitt's (1985: 5) first and oft quoted line from *Political Theology* becomes relevant again at this point: 'Sovereign is he who decides on the exception'. So, how precisely does this relate to the figure of Homo Sacer and to the other concepts sketched out so far? Well, we can start by suggesting that not just anyone can forcibly reduce another person to bare life. In principle, people are equal and possessed of equal rights and personhood. It is illegal in most instances to kill someone, to treat them as animal or to trample on their rights and liberties, be they civil, political or social. However, for Agamben, this doesn't hold fully up and the deviation to this in terms of who may act in ways that might otherwise be seen as unacceptable is the Sovereign, 'he who decides the exception' or, in other words, the person who rules or governs. Historically, the sovereign may have been a king, a queen or another unelected ruler. In modern terms, the Sovereign takes the form of the nation state which can, in certain circumstances, make 'exceptions'; that is, can suspend the rights and liberties of persons, can even incarcerate, punish and perhaps kill persons. While not someone who Agamben drew upon directly, the sociology of Max Weber and particularly his thoughts on monopolistic violence are instructive here. In defining basic sociological terms, Weber (1922/1978: 54) describes the state as:

> A compulsory political organization with continuous operations will be called a 'state' insofar as its administrative staff successfully upholds the claim to the monopoly of the legitimate use of physical force in the enforcement of its order.

What is key in Weber's definition of the state here and where it intersects with Agamben's theory of a state of exception is that Weber identifies that part of what makes a state a state is a monopoly on physical force that can be used to maintain order. This is part of what makes a state sovereign, and this is also identified by Agamben as at least one part of what allows states to create 'exceptions' in carrying out their activities. Effectively, we 'buy into' the fact that states can and do exercise force against people, against us. However, in constitutional democracies, the people are sovereign too and this means that states, though they may have a legitimate monopoly on violence, cannot, in theory, simply go around depriving people of their liberty, maiming, murdering or otherwise reducing people to bare life. Therefore, in order for a state to take these kinds of actions, a state of exception must be created. Moreover, a state of exception must at least have the veneer of legitimacy. To give us a sense of what he means by such a state of exception, Agamben uses the example of the Nazi concentration camps. Using this example, Agamben demonstrates how the Nazi administration constructed a massive state apparatus distributed across a number of camps which were geographically bounded and beyond the borders of which existed a literal state of exception wherein prisoners were forcibly reduced to bare life, to the status of Homo Sacer. Duque Silva and Del Prado Higuera (2021: 503) sum this up in the following terms:

> The individuals in a concentration camp are stripped of all rights and political–legal status; their life is treated, by the agents of power, as matter

without human form, naked life: they are data, figures, biological units that are always disposable.

This is an extreme if not historically unfamiliar example of what Agamben points to as a state of exception. Moreover, though the Nazi concentration camps were in so many ways a precursor to and catalyst for the **Universal Declaration of Human Rights**, for Agamben, the very fact that a state can forcibly reduce a person to bare life in this way recalls the philosophy of Simone Weil in demonstrating the complete inadequacy of human rights as a protection against atrocity. Moreover, this example also evokes Schmitt's critique of constitutional democracies as impractical, inadequate and largely rhetorical. However, for Agamben, the example

> **The Universal Declaration of Human Rights** is an international document adopted by the United Nations General Assembly in 1948 in the wake of the Second World War. Ostensibly, it enshrines the rights and freedoms of all human beings.

of the concentration camp is an example of the state of exception in the purest and most extreme form. It is offered as a jumping-off point to later show how states of exception in veiled and perhaps diluted form persist and, indeed, characterise western liberal democracies. In fact, for Agamben, the Nazi camps effectively become the blueprint for how to govern through the creation of states of exception. If this seems at first far-fetched, it must be remembered that the Nazis did not just strip prisoners of their humanity beyond the walls of the camp but had made a concerted effort to do so and had symbolically and socially rendered Jewish persons, along with Roma and others, as subhuman before a single extermination camp had been constructed. States of exception then have social textures. In fact, for Agamben, states of exception can persist wholly in social forms and in forms that devolve on biopolitics. Duque Silva and Del Prado Higuera (2021: 502) sketch this out in the following terms:

> From Agamben's perspective, the most reprehensible cruelties that have taken place in the exercise of power in the West, instead of being exceptional anomalies, constitute instances inherent in the process of the social construction of modernity. ... Indeed, Auschwitz constitutes the obscene paradigm of the modern that Agamben turns into the founding myth of a biopolitical era. This paradigm refuses to 'remain in the past' and gives meaning to contemporary forms of government.

> **Walter Benjamin** (15 July 1892 to 26 September 1940) was a German Jewish philosopher and cultural critic. A critical theorist in his own right, he was associated with the famous Frankfurt School.

So then, for Agamben, contemporary forms of government proceed by creating states of exception and the structure of the concentration camp, though now much more subtle, is visible in modern political strategies. In many ways, for Agamben, evoking **Walter Benjamin**, the state of exception is no longer to be thought of as something exceptional, as it has more or less become the norm. If we therefore take this example and use it to scrutinise modern society, we should be able to identify states of exception in contemporary form. In this respect, it may be useful to work briefly through some examples before finally relating Agamben's work to social work.

Examples of the state of exception

If we take a state of exception in contemporary form to mean a state or government as declaring some form of a state of emergency and subsequently suspending the rights and liberties of a group or groups of persons, an example that quickly comes to mind is Guantanamo Bay. Located on a US Naval Base in Cuba, Guantanamo Bay is a detention camp that has been and is used to house suspected terrorists in the wake of the 11 September 2001 attacks on the United States by the group identified as Al-Qaeda. Opened in 2002, prisoners are interred there without trial and for unspecified periods. It is also well known that conditions in the detention camp are harsh and inhumane, and that degrading and violent interrogation techniques are permitted and used (see Gregory, 2006). For Agamben, who specifically takes aim at Guantanamo Bay in his 2005 work, *State of Exception*, this provides a concrete example of a state of exception. Moreover, all of Agamben's concepts that have been sketched out so far are present in this example as the *bios* of those interred in Guantanamo is forcibly removed and they are forcibly reduced to bare life and rendered as Homo Sacer. They have no legal status, no recourse to human rights and for Agamben (2005) they have effectively become non-persons whose bodies are ruled over and managed through raw power. While they remain alive biologically, socially and politically they are deceased. This is an example of the political tactic of a state of exception being used so that a group of people can be treated as little more than animals within the confines of specially created (and contested) legal structures. A further, less extreme and perhaps more normalised example (in that it is couched in a much more collective experience) comes in the form of the COVID-19 global pandemic. Mentioned at the outset of this chapter, Agamben was critical of the lockdown measures imposed during the COVID-19 pandemic and directly named the way in which the pandemic was being communicated about as an attempt to create a state of exception. Naming the Italian government's actions as a disproportionate response, Agamben (2020: np) noted that:

> what is once again manifest is the tendency to use a state of exception as a normal paradigm for government. The legislative decree immediately approved by the government 'for hygiene and public safety reasons' actually produces an authentic militarization 'of the municipalities and areas with the presence of at least one person who tests positive and for whom the source of transmission is unknown, or in which there is at least one case that is not ascribable to a person who recently

returned from an area already affected by the virus'. Such a vague and undetermined definition will make it possible to rapidly extend the state of exception to all regions, as it's almost impossible that other such cases will not appear elsewhere.

For Agamben, whose theorising up until then had in large part remained abstract, the COVID-19 pandemic saw much of what he had argued for years manifest in a large-scale global event. While it is difficult to give credence to Agamben's dismissal of the Sars-CoV2 virus as a 'sort of influenza', many of the concepts he used to sketch his arguments *were* arguably visible during the pandemic. The *bios* of persons was suspended in large part at least, people were severely curtailed in their movements, normal liberties were suspended and people were largely and strongly expected to take the vaccines that were offered once these became available. This large-scale control of the bodies of persons happening at the level of populations is arguably indicative of the reduction of persons to bare life while leaving them in the grip of a form of mass biopolitics, thus constituting a state of exception.

Social work and states of exception

How then might we use Agamben's work to think about social work? Arguably, Agamben's work can be used to prompt both critical reflection and to chart positive reform. With respect to critical reflection, we can first consider that social work as a profession that is conducted in multiple contexts and that reflects a specific societal mandate is often concerned with assessment and risk management and that through this process, decisions can be and are made about and for persons in a way that can remove aspects of their *bios*, their political life and reduce them, in part, to *zoë*. The social work process therefore arguably creates or has the potential to create states of exception. In creating such states of exception, the right of persons can be diluted or suspended. We can think about this using the following formula:

- The removal of *bios*:
  - The rights of service users may be suspended, they may be forced to comply.
- The reduction to *zoë*:
  - The most basic processes of their lives may be managed or up for debate.
- States of exception are created:
  - Certain rights, usually available to everyone, are suspended.

This formula can be applied in multiple contexts and with cohorts whom social workers are likely to encounter in areas such as child protection, disability, mental health and elderly care settings and with subject positions such as social class, gender and race. Let's work through a simple example. Arising from child protection concerns, a child is forcibly (against a parent or parents' wishes) and legally (via a court order) removed to care.

- The removal of *bios*:
  - A parent or parents have been forced to comply with a court order. A child has been removed to care and the political right of the parent or parents to care for the child and to make decisions about the child's life has been removed in part. The child's right to reside in the family home has also been rescinded.
- The reduction to *zoë*:
  - In order to seek to have the child returned to their care, the parent or parents must comply with a set of orders. These orders intersect with the bodily autonomy of the parent or parents and might include seeking medical or psychological treatment, providing urine samples, providing evidence of job-seeking activities or educational attainment.
- States of exception are created:
  - In normal circumstances, it a parent's right to care for their child and to manage their child's upbringing. In this example, an exception has been made. In normal circumstances, it is a child's right to remain in their family home. In this example, this right has been rescinded. In normal circumstances, a person will not have to provide urine specimens or show evidence of medical or psychological treatment. In this example, an exception has been made.

While the example laid out is in very simple terms and while children are not removed to care without very valid reasons, the above nevertheless gives a sense of how Agamben's concepts can be used to think about what happens in the social work process and it should be possible to use and apply this formula as a critically reflective tool in multiple contexts. Moreover, this example also demonstrates clear problems with rights-based language in that, though again, there may be good reasons, rights can clearly be suspended and where rights can be suspended for good reasons they can also be potentially suspended for questionable reasons. For Agamben, this paradox at the core of human rights ultimately means a move away from human rights is necessary in order to imagine something new and better as opposed to any attempt at their improvement. In this respect, while what Agamben offers can seem like a deeply pessimistic and dark ontology and the examples he draws upon are couched in the most troubling components of a common humanity, he is also interested in potential and potentiality. Moreover, working with potential is something that social workers are arguably primed to do so that Agamben's challenge can go towards a project of improvement for social work. This may mean rethinking or reframing social work's commitment to human rights while also thinking about ways to foster new forms of inclusion. As noted, for Agamben, human rights as a concept or set of prescriptions can have 'concerning exclusionary effects' (Whelan and Flynn, 2023: 3). Moreover, if we take Agamben's (1998: 113–114) assertion that

> 'the people' that are supposedly the sovereign citizens of the modern state can only be constituted at the exclusion of those who do not belong (i.e. foreigners, dissidents, refugees, people on welfare, drug users, etc.)

this is clearly at odds with the ethos of a social work profession that seeks to value diversity and foster inclusion. However, Ottmann and Silva Brito (2020: 226) reframe Agamben's use of bare life to suggest that it can be seen also be seen as a starting point:

> Ultimately, the authority deciding over who belongs and who does not is the state. By relinquishing the old notions of universal rights, and by starting with bare life, Agamben hopes to create the possibility of a political order without a social division at its core – a people without threshold.

This potential of a 'people without threshold' who are not limited by outdated and antiquated ideas about human rights that leave many out in the cold is also something that interested Agamben. As expected, he couches this interest in a critique; however, this critique suggests that the institutions of the state, of which social work is one, are not oriented towards and don't appear to be interested in the potential of people. Considering potential in a non-prescriptive and very general way, Agamben suggests that society is actually organised in a way that does not value the potential that all people carry; the potential to be and to do many things. If we were to apply this critique to the social work context as part of a project of improvement, this would in many ways mean returning to prominence much of what lies at the core of social work as a project and valuing individuality while also cherishing and caring for the collective. In real terms, this might mean moving away from general assessment and risk management, which sees people as homogeneous and towards approaches which see people as heterogenous, unique and valuable, as laden with potential even where that potential might not become fully actualised. This more integrated, more universal approach to what it means to be human and to share a common humanity arguably holds deep lessons for social work.

Summary

In this chapter, we introduced and examined the work of the philosopher and social theorist, Giorgio Agamben. In particular we focused on his Homo Sacer project and his theory of a state of exception. Following Foucault and drawing inspiration from many quarters including from Simone Weil and Carl Schmitt we saw that Agamben uses a range of concepts to develop his theory. Starting with *zoë* (bare life), *bios* (political life) and subsequently introducing the figure of Homo Sacer, Agamben makes the case that the latter represents a figure from history whose political life has been forcibly removed and who has been reduced to bare life or to the status of an animal. Agamben then transplants this historical figure into the modern nation state in order to elucidate his theory of a state of exception. A state of exception as a political strategy for Agamben models itself on the logic of the Nazi concentration camps wherein the people were reduced to bare life, as people without humanity, and were therefore managed and treated in ways that would be seen as abhorrent and unacceptable under normal circumstances. Agamben extends this analogy outward to critique the nation state in liberal democracies. We also saw that Agamben problematises human rights as inadequate, exclusive and as a sometimes veil for abuses and atrocity. Finally, we saw that Agamben suggests that a move away from rights and towards potential presents a more integrated, inclusive and universal approach to a shared and common humanity.

For students: Exercise box 11

In this chapter we explored the work of Giorgio Agamben, concentrating on his use of the theory of state(s) of exception. To further explore your understanding, consider the following:

1. Do societies create spaces where states of exception exist? Can you think of some? These can be historical or contemporary.
2. Can states of exception be seen in the way some groups are treated?
3. Reflect. Does social work help create or maintain states of exception?

Further reading
- This book represents a reasonably accessible entry point into the work of Agamben:
- de la Durantaye, L. (2009) *Giorgio Agamben: A Critical Introduction*, Stanford: Stanford University Press.
- This journal article uses Agamben's work to interrogate human rights in a social work context:
- Whelan, J. and Flynn, S. (2023). 'Who's right? What rights? How? Rights debates in Irish social work: a call for nuance', *Critical and Radical Social Work*, 12(2): 274–80.

Why not watch!
There are many useful clips on YouTube that may help to flesh out and deepen your understanding. One that is particularly useful is called 'Agamben Homo Sacer animatic' and is published by the Tommie Soro YouTube channel. It is available here: https://youtu.be/pGUxQmRNhtk?si=yGMn3u1IY_4jlQT0

Why not listen!
Podcasts are a great way to learn! The following podcast was produced as part of the Philosophize This! Series of podcasts and provides an excellent and accessible overview of Agamben's work. It is available here: https://www.philosophizet his.org/podcast/episode-179-consciousness-hard-problem-l8d98-td63g-47g5g-ha6yr-papmr-kaj7p-4ybpm-m83zf-6gzkc

Chapter references

Agamben, G. (1998) *Homo Sacer: Sovereign Power and Bare Life*, Stanford, Stanford University Press.

Agamben, G. (2005) *State of Exception*, Chicago: University of Chicago Press.

Agamben, G. (2020) 'The invention of an epidemic', *Quodlibet*, Available from: https://www.quodlibet.it/giorgio-agamben-l-invenzione-di-un-epidemia [Accessed 27 June 2024].

Andrew, E. (1986) 'Simone Weil on the injustice of rights-based doctrines', *The Review of Politics*, 48(1): 60–91.

Duque Silva, G. and Del Prado Higuera, C. (2021) 'Political Theology and COVID-19: Agamben's Critique of Science as a New "Pandemic Religion"', *Open Theology*, 7(1): 501–13.

Gregory, D. (2006). 'The black flag: Guantánamo Bay and the space of exception', *Geografiska Annaler. Series B, Human Geography*, 88(4): 405–27.

Ottmann, G. and Silva Brito, I. (2020) 'Giorgio Agamben: sovereign power, bio-politics and the totalitarian tendencies within societies', in C. Morley, P. Ablett, C. Noble and S. Cowden (eds) *The Routledge Handbook of Critical Pedagogies for Social Work*, Abingdon: Routledge, pp 223–32.

Schmitt, C. (1985) *Political Theology: Four Essays on the Concept of Sovereignty*, translated by George Schwab, Chicago: University of Chicago Press.

Weber, M. (1922/1978) *Economy and Society: An Outline of Interpretive Sociology*, Berkeley: University of California Press.

Weil, S. (1963) 'Human Personality', in *Selected Essays 1934–43*, translated by R. Rees, Oxford: Oxford University Press, p 9.

Whelan, J. (2024). 'Governmentalizing the "social work subject": Social work in Ireland in the era of corporate governance: A sociological analysis', in R. Baikady, J. Przeperski, S.M. Sajid and M.R. Islam (eds) *The Oxford Handbook of Power, Politics and Social Work*, New York: Oxford University Press, pp 775–91.

Whelan, J. and Flynn, S. (2023) 'Who's right? What rights? How? Rights debates in Irish social work: a call for nuance', *Critical and Radical Social Work*, 12(2): 274–80.

For instructors: A set of slides that accompany this chapter can be accessed through the book webpage: https://policy.bristoluniversitypress.co.uk/critical-theory-for-social-work.

12

Summary: revisiting the learning outcomes

In this brief summary, I want to remind the reader of what this text has consisted of while also leaving the reader with some suggestions to help further theorise practice using the work of theorists both featured here and not featured here. To do this, this chapter will work through the learning outcomes that were flagged at the beginning of the text. As a reminder, these are as follows:

- Readers will be able to distinguish between concepts and theory generally.
- Readers will have a good understanding of what generally characterises theory associated with traditional modernity and what characterises theory associated with postmodernity.
- Readers will be able take their understanding of how to use theory to think about social work and apply it to the work of theorists not covered in this text.
- Readers will be able to use the theories and concepts introduced in the text as tools that allow them to reflect deeply on practice.

Learning outcome 1: Readers will be able to distinguish between concepts and theory generally

In the introduction to the book, a way of thinking about the differences between concepts and theories was outlined. Effectively, it was suggested that concepts are the building blocks of theory while also being key components of how we communicate with each other and across languages. This means that we need shared concepts in order to be able to talk to one another. So, if I want to talk to you about driving, we will both need to have the concepts 'car', 'road', 'fuel' and many others. If you and I don't share the same language, as long as we share concepts, we can find a way to communicate. The terms concept and theory are often used interchangeably and for this reason you will find that keeping them distinct can be a difficult task. One way to do this from a social work perspective might be to think of concepts as being more than just an important precursor to thinking theoretically and as thinking and practical tools in their own right. This is an important consideration for social work because it is possible to share a language and concepts with someone while also having very different ways of viewing the world due to very different lived experiences. So, for example, social workers will encounter people who understand the shared concept of education at a surface level and can speak about it. However, if social workers encounter a service user in a family where educational attainment levels are low and where experiences of education have been negative, the shared concept will only go so far, and education may in reality mean very different things to those involved in the conversation. In this scenario, though the social worker and the service user

> **Ludwig Josef Johann Wittgenstein** (26 April 1889 to 29 April 1951) was an Austrian philosopher who worked primarily in logic, the philosophy of mathematics, the philosophy of mind and the philosophy of language.

may both share some understanding of education, they may value it very differently. In this respect, even in cases where a language is shared and a concept is understood in a general way, there can still be difficulty with communication when the experiences of those in dialogue have been very different. The philosopher **Wittgenstein** famously summed this up by saying that if a lion could speak, we could not understand him. What Wittgenstein is saying here is that even if we met a lion who could speak the same language as us, we couldn't possibly hope to hold a conversation with the lion as our range of experiences are so vastly different that the lion would not understand our reality and we would not understand the lion's. So, despite shared language we will struggle to really understand one another if we don't share the same concepts. Moreover, our range of experiences are also key. For example, I could listen to two theoretical physicists conversing in a language I can understand without ever really understanding anything they say. For this reason, when thinking theoretically about practice, or when engaging in practice with people who have had very different lived experiences, starting with a shared concept as a way to understand is crucial. However, working with that concept to move towards a shared and mutual understanding is also just as crucial. Concepts then are the building blocks of theory, but they are also important to everyday communication and therefore to social work.

As further noted in the introduction, where concepts seek to aid understanding, theories seek to illuminate and explain the social world at a range of levels. In social work, theory can be used to help students and practitioners understand what is happening in society, what is happening in the profession of social work or in a specific social work context, along with what is happening in the lives

> **Jean-François Lyotard** (10 August 1924 to 21 April 1998) was a French philosopher and social theorist who is best known for his work *The Postmodern Condition*, which is a key text for understanding the debate surrounding postmodernity.

of the people with whom social workers work. In the introduction, this tendency for theories to operate across a number of levels was explained by distinguishing between 'grand theories', which seek to offer large-scale explanations of social phenomena, 'middle-range theories', which are less grand in scale and seek to explain something reasonably specific and 'micro theories', which are smaller in scale again and might seek to explain something at a very local level. All are important and all will have been encountered here so that we might say that Marx's critique of political economy represents what the philosopher and theorist **Jean-François Lyotard** may have called a 'grand narrative'. Accordingly, many grand theoretical narratives will have their roots in Enlightenment thinking which, as we have seen, sought for higher truths. Equally, we could suggest that the work of Michel Foucault rejects the grand narrative, takes a particular social phenomenon as a focal point (think sex, mental illness, prisons) and strives to theorise a series of middle-range and interrelated theories to arrive at explanation. This rejection of the grand narrative in favour of a tapestry of smaller interconnected theories captures what Lyotard would have called 'little narratives'. What is crucial to understand from the perspective of this book is that whether we seek to use grand narratives or little narratives, when we employ theory critically, we not only seek to understand and explain but also to interrogate, emancipate and disrupt. As noted in the introduction, this is what makes critical theory different to non-critical social theory. Moreover, this is an important consideration for social work and so worth briefly unpacking further. If we proceed on the basis that the people social workers work with are often disadvantaged and can be oppressed, then a critically informed social worker will seek to engage with theories that make connections between the individuals they work with and the social structures that characterise the societies they inhabit. Furthermore, it is through interrogating critical theory with emancipatory potential in the classroom that social workers equip themselves with what is required to engage in critically informed social work practice.

Returning to consider how concepts and theories have been used in this book, we can sketch an example from a theorist who has been covered here. So, we might ask, what is the overarching theory offered by Pierre Bourdieu and what concepts did he develop and deploy to aid understanding? To answer, we might say that Bourdieu was interested in developing a theory of power and of how and why social class reproduces itself. In moving towards developing a theory, Bourdieu developed a range of concepts including habitus, capitals (social, economic, cultural and symbolic) and field. In this simple example, we distinguish in general terms between concepts and theory in a way that readers should be able to take up and apply to other theorists and when thinking about social work. The point here is not to be prescriptive, and this formula may work more or less well depending on the theorist. However, using this formula allows for readers to have a starting point when interrogating theory for social work practice so that, as per the learning outcome, readers will be able to differentiate between theories and concepts generally and use this to approach and understand the work of a range of theorists.

Learning outcome 2: Readers will have a good understanding of what generally characterises theory associated with traditional modernity and what characterises theory associated with postmodernity

In Chapter 2 we looked at the differences between traditional modernity and postmodernity. Here we saw that modernity, if looked at as a phase in human development, was characterised by many constituent parts including the Enlightenment, the Renaissance, the Reformation, the rise of liberal democracy and the Industrial Revolution. With respect to social theory and to what constitutes knowledge and how we can know about the world, the Enlightenment is of particular importance as it ushered in a new approach to knowing – to how you could know and to who could know – and new ideas about things like beauty and truth. Drawing on Howe's (1994) classic essay, we saw that social work as a 'child of modernity' comprised three major cornerstones: care, confront and control, which themselves devolved upon Enlightenment ideas about the good, the beautiful and the true. What is key to remember with respect to this particular learning outcome is that the thought and theory associated with traditional modernity is generally invested in the idea that there is a universal truth that can be sought and potentially known and that is good for all times and in all places, that there is an aesthetic of beauty that surpasses all else and that there are moral and ethical truths and principles that people should generally try to uphold and otherwise live by. In traditional modernity then, there is the possibility of certainty in the world, and this is a certainty in which social work as a project found its initial impetus, developed its knowledge, skills and value base and ultimately became a profession founded on an agreed set of principles. Conversely, the thought and theory associated with postmodernity completely rejects the notion of universality and problematises much of what is associated with Enlightenment thinking. Poststructuralist and postmodern thinkers take aim at modernity's truths with a view to disrupting and deconstructing that which was perhaps previously held sacred or taken for granted. In this respect, there is a rejection of the idea of universal truth, of true beauty and of fixed ethical and moral principles, all of which are seen as being socially and historically contingent and therefore always potentially subject to changes and flux. We also saw that postmodernist thinking holds a challenge for social work, which originally found its rationale in a series of well-articulated and relatively fixed truths which postmodernist thinking suggests are up for debate after all. However, faced with this challenge, we also saw that problematising fixed ways of knowing offers the potential for social work to include more diverse voices and to honour and include multiple ways of knowing so that the deconstruction associated with postmodern thinking can be a strength for social work.

Learning outcome 3: Readers will be able to take their understanding of how to use theory to think about social work and apply it to the work of theorists not covered in this text

Perhaps the key hope for this book is that readers will be able to take what has been offered here, learn from it and apply it elsewhere. This book is not exhaustive and there are many critical social theorists, some mentioned and many who were not, who also have much to offer students and practitioners of social work and the social sciences in general and who have not been covered here. To show how it is possible to use the approach offered in this text to scrutinise the work of other theorists, I will first work through an example based on a theorist that has been covered here as a means of identifying a loose template before working through an example of a theorist who has not featured here at length. The formula that will be used for doing so will take the following form:

1. Major theory: What is the major theory I am interested in?
2. Conceptual buildings blocks: What are the conceptual building blocks?
3. Thinking about social work: How can I use this to think about social work?

Let's start with the last theorist we covered, Giorgio Agamben, who is hopefully fresh in reader's minds. In unpacking Agamben's contribution we saw that he has, building on the work of others, advanced a theory of the state of exception that is ultimately a theory of how states use power and govern by contriving, creating or otherwise using exceptional circumstances to suspend 'normal' social rules and laws. For clarity, let's call this Agamben's theory of the state of exception.

1. Agamben's major theory:
   a. Agamben's theory of the state of exception.

In building towards his theory of a state of exception we saw that Agamben deployed a range of concepts to aid understanding, he drew on the Greek concepts of *zoë* (bare life), *bios* (political life) and Homo Sacer (a person forcibly reduced to bare life).

2. Agamben's conceptual building blocks:
   a. *Zoë* (bare life).
   b. *Bios* (political life).
   c. Homo Sacer (a person forcibly reduced to bare life).

Now we have a sense of both Agamben's overarching theory and the concepts he used to help develop it, we can interrogate how all this might be useful for social work practice.

3. Thinking about social work: How can I use Agamben to think about social work?
   a. Using Agamben's work to think about social work, we saw that the social work process can sometimes remove or suspend the *bios* of persons. We saw that this has implications for rights-based work and for the limitations of rights.

Agamben has been covered extensively in this book so the above will be reasonably familiar. However, we can now take this formula and apply it to the work of theorists not covered here extensively. This of course assumes that you have read and engaged with the work of the theorist or theorists concerned. Let's have a look at the work of Kimberlé Crenshaw who we touched on briefly in the chapter on bell hooks. We can start by saying that, inspired by the work and words of others, Crenshaw formally developed a theory of intersectionality to show how race and sex combined and, indeed, compounded, to enhance the oppression of African-American women.

1. Crenshaw's major theory:
   a. Crenshaw's theory of intersectionality.

In building towards her theory of intersectionality, Crenshaw interrogates how different types of discrimination are viewed and treated separately and how this overtly disadvantages people who face multiple forms of discrimination.

2. Crenshaw's conceptual building blocks:
   a. Discrimination based on gender and race.
   b. The tendency in law for overlapping discriminations to be looked at separately and/or not considered together.

Now that we have a sense of Crenshaw's overarching theory along with the concepts she used to help develop it, we can interrogate how all this might be useful for social work practice.

3. Thinking about social work. How can I use the work of Kimberlé Crenshaw to think about social work?
   a. We can use Crenshaw's work to interrogate whether or not there are two or more forms of discrimination operating in the lives of the people we work with and how this might disadvantage them.
   b. We can interrogate and check our own practice to see if we are actively recognising where different forms of discrimination intersect.

This purpose here is not to be prescriptive, and the steps detailed above can of course be adapted. Moreover, sometimes engaging with the work of theorists and academics will not yield a set of easily identifiable concepts and a theory or theories in which to anchor this particular method and so in cases like this, it is best to simply ask: 'how can I use the work of this theorist to think about social work?' and then take what is useful and leave the rest. Nevertheless, the steps detailed above should equip readers with a very simple template through which to approach critical social theory.

Learning outcome 4: Readers will be able to use the theories and concepts introduced in the text as tools that allow them to reflect deeply on practice

Reflection and reflective practice form core components of social work across jurisdictions. At the outset it was noted that this is a book about thinking as opposed to doing; however, it is hoped that what has been offered here will at the very least aid in the doing by offering tools for reflection. In this respect, the work of any of the theorists covered here can be approached with a view to anchoring reflection in some or all of what has been offered by each. So, for example, when thinking about what constitutes good communication in the social work process, it should be possible to draw on the sociology of Habermas and on his ideas about communicative and strategic action. Moreover, when reflecting on a piece of communication that has taken place in a practice or role play context, Habermas's ideas can be used to interrogate what has taken place by asking questions like: was this good communication characterised by openness and sincerity or was the communication less open and more strategic? What could be improved? Without revisiting every theorist, below are some further examples of how using the theorists covered in this book as an aid to reflection could work:

- Using the work of Karl Marx to aid reflection:
  - Use dialectical reasoning to think about the contradictions that characterise social work.
  - Think about Marx's work on the concept of alienation. Reflect on social work practice. What can alienation do and what can it mean for some of the people with whom social workers work?
- Using the work of Axel Honneth to aid reflection:
  - Use Honneth's work on recognition to think about those who can struggle for recognition and how and what this might mean for their rights and self-worth.
  - Does social work as a discipline always seek to appropriately recognise or can social work misrecognise?
- Use the work of Judith Butler to aid reflection:
  - Use Butler's work on sex and gender as a starting point to think about aspects of identity.
  - How does our view of 'fixed' identities or subject positions shape our expectations? Think about identities rooted in race, class, ethnicity etc.
  - How does social work deal with identity generally? Do social workers have expectations that are dependent on things like gender, class, ethnicity?
  - Can this be problematic?

Used in this way, the work of any or all of the theorists introduced in this book can be adapted to aid reflection. Moreover, the work of theorists who have not been covered here can also be approached in this way. Using the work of critical social theorists to underpin reflection in this way can allow social workers to do the deep reflection that informs and enhances the work so that the thinking informs the doing. In this respect, the Greek lyrical poet, Archilochus is said to have remarked that in challenging circumstances: *We don't rise to the level of our expectations, we fall to the level of our training.* Ultimately then, for social workers, a training and education that is richly, theoretically and critically informed will mean having less distance to fall.

For students: Exercise box 12

In this chapter we summarised the content of the book and offered some suggestions for how to use what has been covered and to take your learning further. To further solidify your learning, complete the following exercise.

1. Take the work of a theorist with whom you are familiar and who has **not** been covered in this book:
   a. What key concepts can you identify?
   b. What overarching theory can you identify?
   c. Is the theorist you have selected more associated with traditional modernity or with postmodernity?
   d. How can you use this work as an aid to reflective practice?

Further reading
- A useful reference source for anyone interested in critical theory is a dictionary of critical theory:
- Macey, D. (2002) *Dictionary of Critical Theory*, London: Penguin.

Chapter reference
Howe, D. (1994) 'Modernity, postmodernity and social work', *British Journal of Social Work*, 24: 513–32.

For instructors: A set of slides that accompany this chapter can be accessed through the book webpage: https://policy.bristoluniversitypress.co.uk/critical-theory-for-social-work.

Index

Note: References to figures appear in *italic* type.

Index

Heidegger, Martin 135
heteronormativity 122, 131
heterosexuality 122, 124
heuristic device 40
Hicks, S. 130
Hirst, Damien 18
The History of Madness (Foucault) 107
The History of Sexuality: Volume One (Foucault) 107
Hobbes, Thomas 138
Homo Sacer 135, 136, 137, 139–40, 147, 155
    and killable bodies 141
    and state of exception 138
Homo Sacer: Sovereign Power and Bare Life
      (Agamben) 135, 136, 139–40, 146–7
Honneth, Axel 67–8, 69–70, 71, 75–6, 129, 157
hooks, bell 93–5, 97–8, 100–4, 105
Horkheimer, Max 4
Houston, S. 55, 56, 58, 59, 71, 80
    on communicative action 61
    on cultural capital 82, 83
    on habitus 86, 87
    on strategic action 62
Howe, D. 9, 15, 18, 21, 154
    on beauty 10–11, 16
    on love 70
human rights 136, 137–8, 143, 146, 147, 148

I

ideal speech situation 61, 63
identity 48, 55, 67, 71, 72
    dual aspects 42, 43, 49
    gender 130–1, 157
    misrecognition 73–4
    and stigma 75
imagination, critical use of 102
income levels 81–2
indigenous knowledges 5
Industrial Revolution 14–15
inequality, and property ownership 81
The Inheritors (Bourdieu and Passeron) 83
Institute for Social Research 3–4, 53
instrumental rationality 56, 62
intersectionality 95–100, 105, 156
Irigaray, Luce 123–4
Irving, A. 107–8, 110, 112
Italian School 136

J

Jim Crow Laws 41

K

Kant, Immanuel 26
Das Kapital (Marx) 30, 31, 32

Kelly, Florence 37
Khan, H. 111
killable bodies 141
King, L. 32
King Junior, Martin Luther 104
Kippax, R. 80
Knickmeyer, R. 29, 30
knowing, ways of 154
knowledge, and power 114–15
Kuhn, Thomas 7

L

Lacan, Jacques Marie Émile 123
Lamentation (The Mourning of Christ) 10, *12*
Lavalette, M. 25, 33–4
Leadbetter, M. 72
Le Guin, Ursula K. 18
lesbianism 124
Leviathan (Hobbes) 138
liberalism 13–14, 15
lifeworld 55–6, 57–8, 59, 61, 62, 63
lockdown 135, 136, 144–5
Long-Acting Reversible Contraceptives
    (LARCs) 115, 127
love 70–1, 75, 102–4, 105
Luther, Martin 13
Lyotard, Jean-François 152, 153

M

Madonna and Child 10, *11*
Maglajlic, R.A. 130–1
Marovatsanga, W. 47
Marshall, T.H. 13–14, 71
Marx, Gary T. 37–8
Marx, Karl 4, 25–8, 29, 34, 152
    and alienation 30–1, 157
    and freedom 32
Mead, George Herbert 61, 68, 69
Merton, Robert 45
microphysics of power 117
micro theory 3, 152
middle-range theory 3, 152
Mills, C. Wright 33
misrecognition 73–5, 76, 129
modernity 8–16, 21, 153–4
'Modernity, Postmodernity and Social Work'
    (Howe) 9
moral appropriateness 60–1, 63
morality 17, 21
Morris, L. 115, 127
Moskowitz, Henry 37
motherhood 127
muckraking 37

Index